Change Your Luck

CHANGE YOUR LUCK

The Scientific Way
to Improve Your Life!

By Dr. Richard Wiseman

American Media, Inc.

CHANGE YOUR LUCK
The scientific way to improve your life!

Copyright © 2003 Dr. Richard Wiseman. Cover copyright © 2004 Miramax Books. All rights reserved.

Cover design: Carlos Plaza
Interior design: Debbie Browning

ISBN: 1-932270-46-9

First printing: 2003 (Hardback)
First paperback printing: December 2004
Printed in the United States of America

10 9 8 7 6 5 4 3 2 1

If an unlucky man sold umbrellas,
it would stop raining;
if he sold candles, the sun would never set;
and if he made coffins, people would stop dying.

—YIDDISH SAYING

Throw a lucky man in the sea and he
will come up with a fish in his mouth.

—ARAB PROVERB

To Caroline

Contents

ACKNOWLEDGMENTS

I would like to thank the following people for their help in conducting the research described here and in writing this book: Dr. Caroline Watt, Dr. Matthew Smith, Dr. Peter Harris, Dr. Emma Greening, Dr. Wendy Middleton, Clive Jeffries, and Helen Large. I am also grateful to the various organizations that helped fund and support this work: the Leverhulme Trust, the University of Hertfordshire, and the BBC. This book would not have been possible without the guidance and expertise of my agent, Patrick Walsh, and editors Kate Parkin and Jonathan Burnham. Finally, my special thanks to the hundreds of lucky and unlucky people who were kind enough to participate in my research and share their fascinating life experiences. In order to preserve their anonymity their names have been changed in this book.

Introduction

Lucky people meet their perfect partners, achieve their lifelong ambitions, find fulfilling careers, and live happy and meaningful lives. Their success is not due to their working especially hard, being amazingly talented, or being exceptionally intelligent. Instead, they appear to have an uncanny ability to be in the right place at the right time and enjoy more than their fair share of lucky breaks. This book describes the first scientific study into why lucky people live such charmed lives and offers ideas for how others can enhance their own good fortune.

The research took several years to complete and involved interviews and experiments with hundreds of exceptionally lucky and unlucky people. The results reveal a radically new way of looking at luck and the vital role that it plays in our lives. People are not born lucky. Instead, lucky people are, without realizing it, using four basic principles to create good fortune in their lives. Understand the principles and you understand luck itself. More important, you can use these principles to enhance the amount of good luck that you experience in your life.

In short, this book presents that most elusive of holy grails—a scientifically proven way to understand, control, and increase your luck.

I have always had a lifelong interest in the remarkable. When I was a child, I became fascinated with magic and illusion. By the time I was ten, I could make handkerchiefs vanish into thin air and thoroughly shuffle a deck of cards without altering their order. In my early teens I joined one of the world's best-known magic societies—The Magic Circle in London. By my early twenties I had been invited to America to perform several times at the prestigious Magic Castle in Hollywood.

I quickly discovered that to be a successful magician you need to understand a great deal about what is going on inside other people's heads. Good magicians know how to distract other people's attention, how to avoid making an audience suspicious, and how to prevent them from working out the correct solution to the trick. As time went on, I became more and more interested in the psychological principles that lay behind the performance of conjuring. Eventually this led me to enroll for a degree in psychology at University College London, and I later studied for my doctorate in psychology at the University of Edinburgh. After Edinburgh, I established my own research unit at the University of Hertfordshire.

At this research unit we have carried out scientific studies into a wide range of psychological phenomena. Perhaps because of my background in magic, I have directed the team to examine areas of psychology that are somewhat unusual.

Some of this work has involved investigating mediums who appear to talk to the dead, psychic detectives who claim to help the police solve crimes, and healers who seem able to psychically cure illness.[1] We have also examined how people's behavior changes when they lie, explored how magicians use psychology to deceive their audiences, investigated ways of detecting lying and deception, and held training courses for people who wish to increase their ability to uncover dishonesty.[2] I have published the findings of this work in scientific journals, presented them at academic conferences, and lectured on their practical applications to the business world.

A few years ago I was asked to give a public talk about my work. I had given many similar talks before but had no idea that this one would radically affect the future direction of my research.

I decided to incorporate a simple magic trick into the talk. I intended to borrow a £10 note from someone in the audience, place it into one of twenty identical envelopes, and mix up the envelopes. I would next ask the person to choose one of the envelopes and then proceed to set fire to the remaining nineteen envelopes. I would then open the one remaining envelope, remove the audience member's money, and congratulate the person on his or her choice.

But the performance that night was slightly odd. I borrowed a note from a woman in the audience, placed it into one of the envelopes, mixed them up, and laid them out in a row. I had kept track of the note and knew that it was in the envelope on the far left. I asked the woman to choose an envelope and was delighted when she chose the envelope that actually contained her money. I gathered up the other envelopes and set fire to them. As the ashes rose into the air, I opened the one remaining envelope and removed the woman's money.

Although the audience laughed and applauded, the woman who had lent me the money didn't look at all surprised. I asked her how she felt about what had happened and she calmly explained that this sort of thing happened to her all the time. She was always in the right place at the right time and had experienced a great deal of good fortune in both her professional and personal life. She said that she wasn't certain why it happened and had always put it down to being lucky.

I was intrigued by her confidence in being lucky and asked if anyone else in the audience thought that they were exceptionally lucky or unlucky. A woman at the front of the auditorium raised her hand and described how her good luck had enabled her to achieve many of her lifetime ambitions. A man at the back of the hall said that he had always been very unlucky and was convinced that if I had borrowed his money then it definitely would have ended up as ash. Only the day before the talk he had bent over to pick up a lucky penny, hit his head on a table and nearly knocked himself unconscious.

After the talk I thought about what had happened. Why should the two women have been especially lucky? And what about the unlucky man? Was he just clumsy, or was there more to his bad luck than that? Was there more to luck than mere chance? I decided to conduct some initial research into the topic. At that time, I had no idea what was ahead of me. I thought that perhaps the research would involve a handful of experiments with a few dozen people. In fact, the project would take eight years to complete and involve working with hundreds of exceptional people.

This book presents the first comprehensive account of my research. I begin by outlining how luck has the power to transform our lives— how a few seconds of good luck can often bring lasting happiness and success, while even a brief encounter with ill fortune can result in failure and despair. I then discuss my initial work on the topic and how this work eventually led to the discovery of the four principles that are at the heart of a lucky life. After discussing each of these principles in detail, I describe techniques and exercises based on these ideas that can be used to create luckier lives.

But before we start, I would like you to answer a few simple questions about yourself.

Your Luck Journal

Throughout the book I am going to ask you to complete various questionnaires and exercises. Many of these are based upon the psychological testing that I carried out during my research with lucky and unlucky people. Please keep a record of your responses in a special "Luck Journal"—a notebook or pad that should be roughly eight inches by six inches, lined, and contain at least forty pages. Your responses will reveal how the various principles of luck relate to you and will help determine the best way for you to enhance the good fortune in your life.

YOUR LUCK JOURNAL: EXERCISE 1

Luck Profile

The first questionnaire is very simple. At the top of the first page in your Luck Journal, please write the heading "Luck Profile." Now draw a vertical line down the center of the page. On the left-hand side of the page write down the numbers 1–12 in a column.

Next, read each of the statements in the Luck Profile questionnaire that follows and write a number between 1 and 5 in the right-hand column to indicate the degree to which you agree or disagree with each statement using the following scale:

1—Strongly disagree

2—Disagree

3—Uncertain

4—Agree

5—Strongly agree

Please read each statement carefully. If you are not certain about the degree to which the statement describes you, simply write down a number that feels most appropriate. Do not spend too long thinking about each statement and answer as honestly as possible.

Luck Profile

Statement	Your rating (1–5)
1 I sometimes chat with strangers when standing in a supermarket or bank line.	_____
2 I do not have a tendency to worry and feel anxious about life.	_____
3 I am open to new experiences, such as trying new types of food or drinks.	_____
4 I often listen to my gut feelings and hunches.	_____
5 I have tried some techniques to boost my intuition, such as meditation or just going to a quiet place.	_____

6　I nearly always expect good
　　things to happen to me in the
　　future.　　　　　　　　　＿＿＿＿＿＿

7　I tend to try to get what I want　＿＿＿＿＿＿
　　from life, even if the chances of
　　success seem slim.

8　I expect most of the people that　＿＿＿＿＿＿
　　I meet to be pleasant, friendly,
　　and helpful.

9　I tend to look on the bright side　＿＿＿＿＿＿
　　of whatever happens to me.

10　I believe that even negative　　＿＿＿＿＿＿
　　events will work out well for me
　　in the long run.

11　I don't tend to dwell on the　　＿＿＿＿＿＿
　　things that haven't worked out
　　well for me in the past.

12　I try to learn from the mistakes　＿＿＿＿＿＿
　　that I have made in the past.

We will return to your answers at various times throughout the book and use them to reveal your personal "Luck Profile"—a unique assessment of how you use luck in your life and, more important, how you can enhance the amount of good fortune that you encounter.

Section One

Initial Research

CHAPTER ONE

The Power of Luck

Entirely too much stress is put on the making of money. That does not require brains. Some of the biggest fools I know are the wealthiest. As a matter of fact, I believe that success is 95 percent luck and 5 percent ability. Take my own case. I know that there are any number of men in my employ who could run my business just as well as I can. They didn't get the breaks—that's the only difference between them and me.[1]

Julius Rosenwald,
past president of Sears, Roebuck and
Company

Luck exerts a dramatic influence over our lives. A few seconds of bad fortune can unravel years of striving, while a moment of good luck can lead to success and happiness. Luck has the power to transform the improbable into the possible; to make the difference between life and death, reward and ruin, happiness and despair.

John Woods, a senior partner in a large legal firm, narrowly escaped death when he left his office in one of the Twin Towers in New York seconds before the building was struck by a hijacked aircraft. This is not the only time that he has been lucky. He was on the thirty-ninth floor of the World Trade Center when it was bombed in 1993, but escaped without injury. In 1988, he was scheduled to be on the Pan Am flight that exploded above Lockerbie in Scotland, but canceled at the last minute because he had been cajoled into attending an office party.[2]

The effects of good and bad luck are not confined to matters of life and death. They can also make the difference between financial reward and ruin.

In June 1980, Maureen Wilcox bought tickets for both the Massachusetts lottery and the Rhode Island Lottery. Incredibly, she managed to choose the winning numbers for both lotteries but didn't win a penny—her Massachusetts numbers won the Rhode Island lottery and her Rhode Island numbers won the Massachusetts lottery.[3] Other lottery players have had the gods of fortune smile on them. In 1985, Evelyn Marie

Adams won $4 million in the New Jersey lottery. Four months later she entered again and won another $1.5 million. Even luckier was Donald Smith. He won the Wisconsin State lottery three times—in May 1993, June 1994, and July 1995—collecting $250,000 each time. The chances of winning this lottery even once are over a million to one.[4]

But it isn't just about the money. Luck also plays a vital role in our personal lives. Stanford psychologist Alfred Bandura has discussed the impact of chance encounters and luck on people's personal lives.[5] Bandura notes both the importance and prevalence of such encounters, writing that "... some of the most important determinants of life paths often arise through the most trivial of circumstances." He supports his case with several telling examples, one of which was drawn from his own life. As a graduate student, Bandura became bored with a reading assignment and so decided to visit the local golf links with a friend. Just by chance, Bandura and his friend found themselves playing behind two attractive female golfers, and soon joined them as a foursome. After the game, Bandura arranged to meet up with one of the women again, and eventually ended up marrying her. A chance meeting on a golf course altered his entire life.

In another example, Bandura described how a simple postal mix-up resulted in Ronald Reagan meeting his future wife Nancy. In the fall of 1949, Nancy Davis noticed her name in a list of Communist sympathizers that had been printed in a Hollywood newspaper. Nancy knew that her name did not belong there and that the mix-up was the result of there being another actress called Nancy Davis. She was concerned about the effect that the listing might have on her career, and so she asked her director to discuss the issue with the then president of the Screen Actors Guild, Ronald Reagan. Reagan assured her director that he understood the situation and that the SAG would defend Nancy Davis if anyone acted against her because they thought she was a Communist. Davis asked to meet with Reagan to discuss the issue further. The two of them met, quickly fell in love, and before long, were married to each other. One lucky meeting changed their lives forever.

A number of researchers have also discussed the effect of good and bad fortune on people's choice of career and success in their professional lives.[6] Once again, they have noted how the impact of these factors is often far from trivial, with many people reporting how chance meetings and lucky opportunities frequently led to a significant shift in career direction or a dramatic promotion. Indeed, the powerful effect of good and bad fortune on people's professional lives has caused one of America's leading career counselors to remark:

> Each one of us could tell stories of how crucial, unplanned events have had a major career impact and how untold thousands of minor unplanned events have had at least a small impact. Influential unplanned events are not uncommon; they are everyday occurrences. Serendipity is not serendipitous. Serendipity is ubiquitous.[7]

These types of factors have certainly influenced my own career. When I was eight I was asked to complete a school project on the history of chess. Being a diligent young student, I decided to pay a visit to my local library to find some books on the topic. Quite by chance, I was directed to the wrong shelf and came across some books on conjuring. I was curious, and started to read all about the secrets that magicians use to achieve the impossible. This was my first introduction to the world of magic, and it influenced the whole of my life. I have no idea what might have happened if I had been directed to the correct shelf and found the chess books. Perhaps I wouldn't have developed an interest in magic, trained as a psychologist, or conducted the research described in this book.

Luck has also exerted a considerable influence on the careers of many highly successful businesspeople.

By the end of his career, Joseph Pulitzer was an extraordinarily successful businessman and philanthropist. He owned one of the largest newspapers in America, helped raise money to fund the pedestal on which the Statue of Liberty now stands, and endowed the world-famous Pulitzer Prize for writing. Yet all of this might never have happened if it weren't for just one lucky break. Pulitzer was born in Hungary. As a young man he suffered from both poor health and extremely bad eyesight. When he was seventeen, he came to America as a penniless immigrant but found it difficult to find employment. As a result, Pulitzer spent a great deal of time playing chess in his local library. On one such visit he happened to meet an editor of a local newspaper. This chance encounter resulted in Pulitzer being offered a job as a junior reporter. After four years he was given the opportunity to buy shares in the paper and jumped at the offer. It was a shrewd decision—the paper proved highly successful and Pulitzer made a considerable profit. Pulitzer continued to make highly successful decisions throughout his life, and he became an editor, and eventually owner, of two of the best-known newspapers of his day. By the end of his career, the man who had started his working life as a poor immigrant had become one of the most influential people in America. His entire career might have taken a completely different direction had it not been for a chance meeting in the chess room of his local library.[8]

Many other businesspeople have also put much of their success down to chance meetings and good luck. Take, for example, the case of Barnett Helzberg Jr. By 1994 Helzberg had built up a chain of highly successful American jewelry stores with an annual revenue of around $300 million. One day he was walking past the Plaza Hotel in New York when he heard a woman call out "Mr. Buffett" to the man next to him. Helzberg wondered whether the man might be Warren Buffett—one of the most successful investors in America. Helzberg had never met Buffett but had read about the financial criteria that Buffett used when buying a company. Helzberg had recently turned sixty, was thinking of selling his company, and realized that his might be the type of company that would interest Buffett. Helzberg seized the opportunity, walked over to the stranger, and introduced himself. The man did indeed turn out to be Warren Buffett and the chance meeting proved highly fortuitous because about a year later Buffett agreed to buy Helzberg's chain of stores. And all because Helzberg just happened to be walking by as a woman called out Buffett's name on a street corner in New York.[9]

And how did Buffett get to be one of the richest men in America? In an interview in *Fortune* magazine, Buffett explained the important role that luck had played early on in his career. When he was twenty, Buffett was rejected from Harvard Business School. He immediately went to a library and began looking into the possibility of applying to other business schools. It was only then that he noticed that two business professors whose work he admired both taught at Columbia. Buffett applied to Columbia at the last minute and was accepted. One of the professors later became Buffett's mentor and helped initiate his highly successful career in business. As Buffett later remarked, "Probably the luckiest thing that ever happened to me was getting rejected from Harvard."

The important role that luck plays in people's careers is not limited just to the world of business.

In 1954, Shirley MacLaine was an unknown actress and had accepted a small part in the chorus of a new musical. She was asked to understudy for the star of the show, Carol Haney, but never rehearsed for the part because Haney had a reputation for going on with the show, regardless of illness or injury. The show opened and Haney received rave reviews. MacLaine was considering giving her notice and taking a part in another show. Then, one night she arrived at the theater and was told that Haney had broken her ankle and simply could not perform. MacLaine was asked to take over the lead. Despite a lack of rehearsal, MacLaine rose to the occasion and received a great reaction from the audience. The following night Hal Wallis, a well-known Hollywood producer, was in the audience and offered her a seven-year contract. Soon afterward, a representative of Alfred Hitchcock saw MacLaine and offered her a part in a forthcoming Hitchcock film.[10]

MacLaine is far from the only celebrity to have her career launched through luck. In 1979, Hollywood producer George Miller was looking for a battle-weary, scarred, tough guy to play the lead in the movie *Mad Max*. The night before his audition, Mel Gibson, then an unknown and sensitive-looking Australian actor, was attacked on the street by three drunks. He arrived for the audition looking beaten and tired, and Miller immediately offered him the part.[11] British supermodel Kate Moss was equally fortuitous. In the early 1990s she was on vacation with her father. The two of them were standing in a check-in line at JFK Airport when a talent scout walked past and noticed her striking looks. Moss went on to become one of the world's most successful and sought-after models—and all because of a lucky chance encounter.[12]

And luck does not determine the success of just actors and models—it even affects the careers and success of scientists and politicians.

Perhaps the most famous example of such scientific serendipity is Sir Alexander Fleming's discovery of penicillin. In the 1920s, Fleming was working to develop more effective antibiotics. Part of his work involved the microscopic examination of bacteria that had been artificially grown in flat glass containers known as petri dishes. Fleming inadvertently left one of the petri dishes uncovered, and a piece of mold fell into the dish. By chance, the mold contained a substance that killed the type of bacteria in the dish. Fleming noticed the effect of the mold, was intrigued, and worked hard to identify the substance responsible for killing the bacteria. He eventually discovered the antibiotic and named it penicillin. Fleming's chance discovery has saved countless lives and has been hailed as one of the biggest advances in the history of medicine.

YOUR LUCK JOURNAL: EXERCISE 2

The Role of Luck in Your Life

On a new page in your Luck Journal, write down a number between 1 and 7 to indicate the degree to which you think luck has influenced your life using the following scale:

Not at all   A great deal
1   2   3   4   5   6   7

Now, underneath, jot down a few brief sentences describing

- how you met your partner

- how you came to know your closest friend

- the main factors that have influenced your choice of career

- a major event that had a positive effect on your life

Next, think about how good luck influenced these events. Think about how tiny changes—such as not going to a certain party or reunion, turning left instead of right, not opening a magazine to a certain page, or not returning a phone call—could have affected these events and perhaps even changed the whole course of your life.

Finally, return to the question about the role that luck has played in your life in regard to these events and answer it a second time. Write down a number between 1 and 7 to indicate the degree to which you now think that luck has influenced your life.

When most people carry out this exercise they realize how important luck has been to them in their lives, and write down a larger number the second time they answer the question.

In fact, chance events and accidental discoveries have frequently altered the course of science and have played an important part in many famous discoveries and inventions, including the contraceptive pill, X-rays, photography, safety glass, artificial sweeteners, Velcro, insulin, and aspirin.[13]

The role of luck in politics is illustrated in the career of President Harry Truman. As a young man, Truman experienced a great deal of ill fortune. He intended to go to college after graduating from high school, but his father lost almost everything in a bad business venture, and so Truman was forced to spend his formative years plowing his grandfather's farm. Soon after World War I he started a clothing store in Kansas City, but again experienced bad luck when he was made bankrupt during the recession. It was not until his late thirties that he obtained his first lucky break—a friend encouraged him to run as county judge and he unexpectedly won the contest. When he was forty-two, he ran for presiding judge and once again won. A few years later, he was nominated for the U.S. Senate and again won. In 1944, the Democrats dropped the then vice president Henry Wallace and nominated Truman as a running mate to Franklin D. Roosevelt. Then, just eighty-two days into his new term, Roosevelt unexpectedly died, making Truman president. Truman's good luck continued throughout his presidency—he pulled off one of the biggest upsets in American political history by beating Thomas E. Dewey in the 1948 presidential election and, just a few years later, survived an assassination attempt by two Puerto Rican nationalists. In his memoirs, Truman wrote: "Popularity and glamour are only part of the factors involved in winning elections. One of the most important of all is luck. In my case, luck was always with me."[14]

In short, luck plays a hugely significant role in many different aspects of our lives. Luck has the power to transform both our personal and professional lives. To many, this is a terrifying idea. Most people like to think that they are in control of their future. They try hard to obtain certain outcomes and avoid others. But, to a large extent, this feeling of control is an illusion. Luck makes a mockery of even our best intentions. It has the power to change everything, within seconds, for better or worse. And it can do so any time, any place, and without warning.

For over a hundred years, psychologists have studied how our lives are affected by our intelligence, personality, genes, appearance, and upbringing. There can be little doubt that the work has yielded considerable insight into the human condition. Yet, despite the enormity of the effort, very little work has examined good and bad luck. I suspect that psychologists have avoided the topic because they prefer, quite understandably, to examine factors they can measure and control more easily. Measuring intelligence and categorizing people's personalities is relatively straightforward, but how do you quantify luck and control chance?

The situation is akin to the old story of the man who knows he dropped some treasure in one part of the street but searches in another part because the light is better there. Psychologists have chosen not to investigate luck because it is much easier to examine other topics. But I have always been interested in trying to examine unusual areas of psychology, areas that other researchers tend to avoid. The result is that I have often found treasure in places that other people have ignored.

In the Introduction to this book I described how I became interested in luck after hearing about how important it had been in the lives of people who attended one of my talks. Soon after that talk I decided to conduct some initial research into the topic. I began by carrying out a survey to discover the percentage of people who considered themselves lucky or unlucky, and whether people's luck tended to be concentrated in one or two areas of their lives or spread across many different areas. Together with a group of my students, I visited the center of London at different times over the course of a week and asked a large number of randomly chosen shoppers about the role of luck in their lives. There were two parts to the survey. First, we asked them whether they considered themselves lucky or unlucky—that is, whether seemingly chance events in their lives had consistently tended to work out in their favor or against them. Second, we asked them whether they had been lucky or unlucky in eight different areas of their lives, including their careers, relationships, home life, health, and financial matters.

We surveyed a very wide range of people—men and women, old and young. The results revealed that 50 percent of people indicated that they had been consistently lucky and a further 14 percent said that they had been consistently unlucky. In other words,

> "Somewhere along the line I made the switch and was able to look at the bright side rather than the dark side all the time. Now I look at everything and think how lucky I am."
>
> —MICHELLE PFEIFFER

64 percent, or nearly two-thirds, of the people questioned indicated that they were consistently lucky or unlucky. Interestingly, there was a very strong tendency for people who said that

they had been lucky in one area of their lives to indicate that they had also been lucky in several others. People who were lucky in their financial lives also reported being lucky in their home lives, and people who were unlucky in their careers were also unlucky in their relationships.[15]

This simple survey showed that most people were indicating an amazing level of consistency in their experience of good and bad luck.

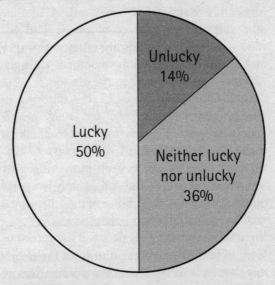

Percentages of people who consider themselves unlucky, lucky, and neither lucky nor unlucky in my initial survey.

Certain people seemed able to consistently attract good luck while others were a magnet for ill fortune. Interestingly, most of the people we interviewed were convinced that their good and bad luck was simply the result of pure chance. Lucky people just happened to live lives that were peppered with chance encounters—such as meetings with loved ones and business colleagues—that always worked out for the best. The unlucky people thought that accidents and ill fortune came their way also by chance alone. I was far from convinced. A lifetime studying the psychology of magic had led me to realize that things are often not as they appear, and that reality is sometimes stranger, and more interesting, than the illusion.

Luck could not simply be the outcome of chance events. There were too many people consistently experiencing good and bad luck for it all to be chance. Instead, there must be something *causing* things to work out consistently well for some people and consistently badly for others. Given the importance of luck, it seemed vital to try to understand why this was the case. Were these people really destined to succeed or fated to fail? Were they part of some huge, cosmic game plan? Were they using some form of psychic ability to create good and bad luck? Or could it all be explained in terms of differences in their beliefs and behavior? Most important of all, if we understood more about what was happening, would it be possible to enhance people's luck?

My survey had raised many interesting questions. I set out to find some answers.

CHAPTER TWO

Lucky and Unlucky Lives

The results of my survey had demonstrated that a majority of people consider themselves consistently lucky or unlucky, and that their good or bad luck was spread across many different areas in their lives. These findings made me eager to discover more about the nature of luck.

I decided that the best way forward would be to carry out some scientific research with groups of exceptionally lucky and unlucky people. This approach is frequently used by psychologists. To find out about how our memories work, researchers might examine people who are especially good or bad at remembering things. Important discoveries about hand-eye coordination have been made by studying top athletes and jugglers. Some of the mysteries of everyday vision have been unraveled by working with both skilled artists and the blind. But I knew that finding exceptionally lucky and unlucky people who would be willing to take part in research would be far from easy. It wasn't even obvious where to start looking.

Fortunately, a few journalists had heard about the survey that I had carried out in London and approached me concerning the possibility of writing articles about my work for various newspapers and magazines. I asked them to mention that I was intending to carry out some additional research into the topic and would like to hear from lucky and unlucky people interested in participating. Every article published resulted in a few more calls to the laboratory, and I slowly started to put together a group of lucky and unlucky volunteers. Over the course of the last eight years, this group has been supplemented by other exceptionally lucky and unlucky people who heard about my research on television programs and radio items, and via the Internet. Together, they represent an extraordinary group of several hundred men and women. The youngest is an eighteen-year-old student, the oldest is an eighty-four-year-old retired accountant. They are drawn from all walks of life—businessmen, academics, factory workers, teachers, housewives, doctors, computer analysts, secretaries, salespeople, and nurses. All were kind enough to let me put their lives and minds under the microscope. I have conducted lengthy interviews with many of them and asked others to keep diaries. Some have been invited to my laboratory to take part in experiments, and others have been asked to complete complicated psychological questionnaires. The research has produced a huge amount of information. With the help of this exceptional group of people, I have slowly uncovered the secret of luck.

Living With Luck

One of my first goals was to discover what it is like to live a lucky or unlucky life. I decided to interview participants about key events in their lives, and their stories provided remarkable evidence about the power of good and bad fortune.

Jodie is a thirty-six-year-old poet from Texas. She considers herself very lucky, as chance encounters have often helped her to achieve many of her dreams. A few years ago, Jodie decided to follow her heart and change her life. From an early age, Jodie had wanted to be a writer and poet. She searched the Internet and came across an organization holding a summer conference that promoted and encouraged women writers. Jodie instantly liked the environment at the conference and thought that she would love to teach there. A few days later, Jodie bumped into the founder of the organization, started chatting, and mentioned that she lived in Texas. The founder said that the organization would be staging a one-day conference there and asked Jodie if she would like to hold a workshop. The event went very well and Jodie was invited to teach at another upcoming conference.

Jodie also came across another Web site that contained news about poetry events in cities across America. She noticed that no one was reporting from Texas, and so she started to submit material. As a result, she began regular e-mail contact with Bill, the site's organizer. One day at a poetry reading in New York, Jodie happened to meet Bill. During their conversation Bill asked whether she could come to New York to help coordinate a series of forthcoming poetry events. Jodie was excited at the opportunity. The only downside was that she had nowhere to live in New York. She mentioned this to Bill, and he sent out a message to everybody on his e-mail list. Within days, Jodie received an e-mail from a woman offering her a room in a great neighborhood at a very low rent. Jodie moved to New York and now earns her living as a poet and writer.

Jodie explained the effect of good fortune on her life:

I have exceptional good luck and it has

helped me achieve many of the most cherished and important aspects of my life. I feel totally in control. Everything that I want to happen has happened. And once I decided I wanted a new direction, it all happened very quickly. It's amazing.

Life for Susan, age thirty-four, is very different. Susan's bad luck started at an early age. As a child she once split her head open on a rock while picking daisies, had to be rescued by firemen when she trapped her foot in a grid, and was hit on the head by a board that fell from the front of a building. But Susan's bad luck was not confined only to her younger years. As an adult, she is unlucky in love. She once arranged to meet a man on a blind date, but he had a motorcycle accident on the way to their meeting and broke both of his legs. Her next date walked into a glass door and broke his nose. The church in which she was due to get married was burned down by arsonists two days before her wedding.

Susan had also experienced an amazing catalogue of accidents. Often, the accidents were far from trivial. On one occasion, she fell and broke her arm. Shortly afterward a second fall resulted in a broken leg. On her driving test she crashed through a wall and then had to pay for the damages to the car as it had not been properly insured.

Driving has continued to present problems. In one especially bad run of luck she reported having more than eight car accidents in a single journey of less than fifty miles. In one interview, Susan tearfully explained: "Not many people want to get in a car with me, and if I go to someone's house, I am told to sit there and not move."

Interviewing unlucky people like Susan often made me feel sad. They were clearly trying their best to live happy and productive lives, but fate always seemed to conspire against them. The situation was quite different when I spoke to lucky people. Their good fortune often seemed continuous and had helped them lead happy and successful lives.

One of the luckiest people to participate in my research was forty-two-year-old sales and marketing manager Lee. Lee has consistently encountered good fortune throughout the whole of his life. When he was just sixteen, Lee agreed to help out on a local farm in the rural community where he was raised. He was sitting on the back of a stationary tractor that was connected to a large automated plow—a fearsome device designed to rip up the soil prior to seeding. A friend decided to take the tractor for a short trip. What he didn't realize was that the movement of the tractor was pushing Lee forward, and onto the moving spikes. In one interview, Lee explained what happened next:

I couldn't grab hold of anything. To my right and left were the fast-moving wheels of the tractor. I realized I was going to fall, and remember looking to my right and left and thinking I can't jump because it's too wide. I was convinced that all the spikes were going to rip me to pieces. At the moment that I started to fall into the actual plow there was a sudden jolt and I was flung backward. The stainless steel link between the tractor and the plow had suddenly sheared. The boss had no idea why it had happened—he had only bought it the previous week. I thought to myself, "My God, Lee, you've been lucky." And that has always stayed with me.

Lee's father was a landscape gardener, and as a young man Lee would often help him out at work. Lee's father once asked him to help out on a particularly difficult job. Lee didn't really want to go, but felt that he should. He went along, met the woman of his dreams, and instantly fell in love. Lee knew that they were made for each other. And his gut feeling proved to be uncannily accurate—the two of them have been happily married for more than twenty-five years.

Lee has also been very lucky in business and

believes that luck has played a significant part in this success:

> I've been in sales and marketing for over twenty years, and at the moment I am a marketing manager for a substantial chain of stores that sell educational toys. I've won lots of awards and promotions, and obtained some senior jobs due to my performance. Luck has played a very, very, significant part in my success. I always seem to be in the right place at the right time. I don't know what draws me to a particular company when they're just screaming out for something that I've got to offer, but it happens to me all the time.

Lee's luck has brought both him and his company a large amount of financial success. Other participants in my research have not been so fortunate. Take the case of fifty-four-year-old small press publisher Stephen from New York. Stephen has experienced financial bad luck throughout his life. Sometimes his ill fortune has been relatively trivial, other times it has had far more serious consequences.

Stephen once believed that he had won a vast amount of money on a scratch card in a daily draw. But a printer's error had resulted in over

Lynne and the Luck of the Draw

Lynne's luck started when she happened to come across a newspaper article describing how a woman had won several impressive competition prizes. Lynne decided to enter a crossword competition and won $25. A few weeks later she entered another competition and won three sports bikes. Shortly afterward, she went to an interview for a position teaching an evening class in fashion design at a local adult learning center. There was a coffee jar on the interviewer's desk and it had a competition entry form on it. Lynne was drawn to this and asked whether she could have the label. The interviewer asked why she wanted it and Lynne told her about how she had won some competitions. The interviewer asked her to come and teach two evening classes—one on fashion design and one on how to win competitions. Lynne accepted the offer and also started to enter many more competitions. Her winning streak continued and she won more prizes, including two cars and several trips to Greece and Italy.

Interestingly, these competition wins allowed Lynne to achieve her lifelong ambition of becoming a freelance writer. In 1992 she wrote a book on winning competitions. To publicize the book, a press release was sent to her local newspaper and they published an article about her work. The next day, the story was picked up by the national newspapers and she was invited to appear on several television shows. As a result, Lynne was invited to write newspaper articles on winning competitions. In 1996 she received a telephone call from a major daily newspaper. They had seen her work and asked her to write a daily competition column for them. Her column, "Win with Lynne," was highly successful and ran for many years.

Lynne has fulfilled many of her lifelong ambitions, has been happily married for more than forty years, and has a wonderful family life. Like many people involved in my research, Lynne attributes much of her success to good fortune.

thirty thousand people all winning the same prize, and so each claimant won only a few dollars. Stephen inherited a very large number of shares in a well-known company. A short while later, the stock market unexpectedly suffered one of its worst ever crashes, and overnight, the shares became almost worthless.

Stephen once rented out some spare office space to a lawyer who offered to help look after Stephen's company's legal work. For the first few months everything went well, but then Stephen started to receive demands for unpaid bills. He eventually discovered that the lawyer had not been paying the bills and had instead been helping himself to company funds. Stephen worked hard to keep the small business afloat, but the stress eventually took its toll on his health. Despite having no previous history of illness, Stephen suffered a very serious heart attack and was forced to declare bankruptcy. He has been unemployed ever since.

Stephen explained to me:

Now I haven't got a business and I haven't got any money. I've always given 101 percent, and I sometimes feel that somebody up there could have given me a better chance. ... I think I deserve better than I've been given, but I guess that's the way the cards have been dealt.

I interviewed hundreds of lucky and unlucky participants and then reviewed their comments to discover consistent ways in which good and bad fortune had influenced their lives. This research revealed that there are four main differences between the lives of lucky and unlucky people:

1. Lucky people constantly encounter chance opportunities. They accidentally meet people who have a very beneficial effect on their lives and come across interesting opportunities in newspapers and magazines. In contrast, unlucky people rarely have these sorts of experiences, or, as in the case with Stephen, they meet people who have a negative effect on their lives.

2. Lucky people make good decisions without knowing why. They just seem to know when a business decision is sound or someone shouldn't be trusted. Unlucky people's decisions tend to result in failure and despair.

3. Lucky people's dreams, ambitions, and goals have an uncanny knack of coming true. Once again, unlucky people are the exact opposite—their dreams and ambitions remain little more than an elusive fantasy.

4. Lucky people have an ability to turn their bad luck into good fortune. Unlucky people lack this ability and their bad luck causes nothing but upset and ruin.

The differences between the two groups were striking. But why should this be the case? Why should everything work out for one group but not for the other?

Some writers have speculated that perhaps lucky and unlucky people might be using some form of psychic ability to create the good and bad fortune in their lives.[1] It is easy to see why they have made this suggestion. Take the cases of Susan and Lynne. Perhaps lucky people, like Lynne, win competitions because, without realizing it, they are able to psychically predict the winning entry. Perhaps Susan is equally psychic but is using her abilities in a self-destructive way, always causing events to work out against her.

It was an interesting idea, and one that had to be properly investigated. But finding out whether lucky people are more psychic than unlucky people is far from easy. I needed to arrange a situation wherein a very large number of exceptionally lucky and unlucky people would be asked to predict the outcome of a random event.

YOUR LUCK JOURNAL: EXERCISE 3

The Luck Questionnaire

My colleagues and I devised a simple questionnaire to reliably classify participants as either lucky, unlucky, or neutral (that is, neither lucky nor unlucky).[2] I have included a version of this questionnaire here. Please take a few minutes to read it, write your scores in your Luck Journal, and then discover how you would be categorized.

To complete the questionnaire, simply read each of the descriptions that follow and, for each one, rate how well it describes you by assigning a number between 1 and 7 on the following scale:

Doesn't   1   2   3   4   5   6   7   Describes me
describe   very well
me at all

Lucky description: Lucky people are people for whom seemingly chance events tend to work out consistently in their favor. For example, they seem to win more than their fair share of raffles and lotteries, or often accidentally meet people who can help them in some way, or their good fortune might help them achieve their ambitions and goals.

How well does this describe you? _____

_____

_____

_____

_____

_____

Unlucky description: Unlucky people are the opposite: Seemingly chance events tend to work out consistently against them. For example, they never seem to win anything in competitions, or they tend to be involved in accidents that are not their fault, or they are unlucky in love, or they experience a great deal of ill fortune in their careers.

How well does this describe you? _____

_____

_____

_____

_____

Scoring:

People are classified as lucky, unlucky or neutral on the basis of their answers. The classification is simple. Just create a luck score by subtracting the rating that you have given to the **unlucky description** from the rating that you have given to the **lucky description**. Thus, if you gave 5 to the first description and 1 to the second, you would have a luck score of +4. If, however, you had given 2 to the first description and 7 to the second, you would have a luck score of -5. Alternatively, if you gave 5 to the first description and 4 to the second, you would have a luck score of +1.

If your luck score is equal to 3 or more, then you would be classified as lucky, if it is equal to -3 or less then you would be classified as unlucky. People obtaining all other luck scores are classified as neutral (that is, neither lucky nor unlucky). Thus, luck scores of +4, -5, and +1 would be classified as lucky, unlucky, and neutral, respectively.

Luck and the Lottery

Shortly after I started my research, I received a call from a television producer who was putting together a new prime-time science program and was keen to make it interactive. He didn't want viewers just to watch, he wanted them to actually take part. I arranged a meeting with my then research assistant, Matthew Smith, and another psychologist who had become interested in studying luck, Dr. Peter Harris, and a very simple solution occurred to us—why not ask lucky and unlucky viewers to try to predict the winning numbers in the UK National Lottery? It was perfect. We would have millions of viewers, and so any appeal for people who were especially lucky or unlucky would result in a large number of participants. The lottery draw was totally random, and people would be highly motivated to do well.

An estimated 13 million viewers tuned in to the program. Toward the end of the show the producers ran a short film about the Luck Project. They had contacted both Susan and Lynne, and presented short profiles of their lives. They also appealed for anyone who thought that he or she was especially lucky or unlucky, and intended to play the National Lottery that week, to get in contact. We expected a few hundred people to phone. Within minutes, we had received an estimated 1 million calls.

We sent the first 1,000 callers a simple form. Playing the UK National Lottery involves buying a ticket and selecting six different numbers between 1 and 49. Each ticket costs £1 and people are free to buy as many tickets as they like. On our form we asked everyone to complete a short questionnaire that would allow us to categorize them as either lucky or unlucky (see Exercise 3), and to tell us which numbers they intended to choose for the forthcoming lottery.

The lottery forms were returned remarkably quickly. The draw was just days away and so we had to act quickly. In all, just over 700 people sent in replies. Among them they intended to buy more than 2,000 lottery tickets. Having processed the data, just one day before the draw, we realized that we had collected some extraordinary information.

Imagine that there really is a link between luck and psychic ability, that lucky people really do pick more winning lottery numbers than unlucky people. If that were the case, then the numbers that were being chosen by the lucky people, but not by the unlucky ones, would be more likely to be winning numbers. Thus, to find the winning lottery numbers, all you would have to do is find out which numbers were being both chosen by lucky people and avoided by unlucky people. It hadn't occurred to us before, but if the theory was right, the data we had collected for our experiment could make us millionaires.

We debated the ethics of the situation. Seconds later, we started to analyze the data. We noticed that some numbers were being chosen by lucky people and avoided by unlucky people. Often the differences were small, but nevertheless, potentially vital. We carefully examined the data and came up with our best shot at the winning numbers: 1, 7, 17, 29, 37, and 44. For the first and only time in my life, I bought a lottery ticket.

The UK National Lottery draw takes place every Saturday night and is broadcast live on prime-time television. As usual, the forty-nine balls were placed in a rotating drum, and six balls, plus a special "bonus" ball, were randomly selected. The winning numbers were 2, 13, 19, 21, 45, and 32. I hadn't managed to match a single number.

But had the lucky and unlucky people in our experiment fared any better? Out of our 700 participants, only 36 won any money at all. These were evenly split between lucky and unlucky people. Just two people managed to match four numbers, winning £58 each. One of these had previously classified themselves as lucky, the other as unlucky. On average, both lucky and unlucky people had bought three tickets, matched one number on each ticket, and lost about £2.50.[3]

YOUR LUCK JOURNAL: EXERCISE 4

Life Satisfaction and Luck

Life Satisfaction Questionnaire

This exercise is all about how satisfied you are with your life right now. On a new page in your Luck Journal please write down the following headings in a column:

My life in general

My family life

My personal life

My financial situation

My health

My career

Now, next to each heading, please write a number between 1 and 7 to indicate how satisfied you are with this particular aspect of your life using the following scale:

Completely   Completely
dissatisfied   satisfied

1   2   3   4   5   6   7

Scoring:

Previous work using this type of questionnaire has found that people's level of life satisfaction is relatively stable over time and is related to their levels of happiness and quality of life.[4]

Add up your scores and then use the following scale to discover whether your level of life satisfaction is low, medium, or high.

Low scores are between 6 and 26.

Medium scores are between 27 and 32

High scores are between 33 and 42

During my research I gave this questionnaire to two hundred lucky, unlucky, and neutral people. The results are shown in the following graph.[5] Lucky people are far more satisfied with all areas of their lives than unlucky and neutral people. The unlucky people were consistently the most dissatisfied.

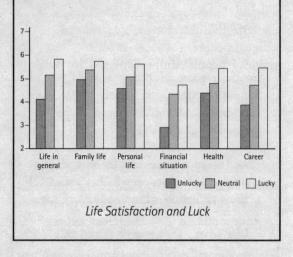

Life Satisfaction and Luck

The experiment had involved hundreds of people who had considered themselves lucky and unlucky. The lottery draw was completely random and unpredictable. Everyone would have been highly motivated to win. If lucky people were more psychic than unlucky people, then they should have matched more numbers and won more money. In the end, lucky people fared no better or worse than unlucky people. Almost everyone who had taken part in the experiment, including me, lost a small amount of money. The results indicated that luck was not due to psychic ability.

Apart from psychic ability, what else might explain the difference between lucky and unlucky people? I wondered whether lucky and unlucky people simply differed in terms of intelligence. Perhaps people like Jodie and Lee are simply more intelligent than people like Susan and Stephen, and this was causing them to be more successful in life. I decided to find out if this was the case by having people complete the Luck Questionnaire and undertake tests that measured two different kinds of intelligence. These intelligence tests have been used in thousands of psychological experiments throughout the world, and they predict how well people will do at school and college, and in certain kinds of jobs. The tests measured participants' nonverbal and verbal reasoning abilities. I calculated the number of correct answers and compared the scores of lucky and unlucky people. Both groups obtained roughly the same scores on both tests of intelligence.[6] I then compared the scores of lucky and unlucky people with the scores of neutral people. Once again, there were no differences. The results of the experiment were clear—being lucky and unlucky is not related to intelligence.

Toward the Four Principles

Although my research had shown that luck was not connected to psychic ability or intelligence, I began to wonder how people's minds might influence their luck in other ways. Do lucky and unlucky people approach life in the same way, and if not, were different viewpoints responsible for creating the positive and negative events in their lives? Luck is generally thought to be an external force: Sometimes we are lucky, sometimes unlucky. But what if we create our own luck? What if, to a very large extent, lucky and unlucky people are responsible for much of the good and bad fortune they encounter?

A clue to the answer came from the lottery experiment. The forms used in the study had asked people about their expectations about winning the lottery. Everyone was asked to rate their confidence of winning something in the lottery that week by circling a number between 1 and 7, where 1 indicated that they were not at all confi-

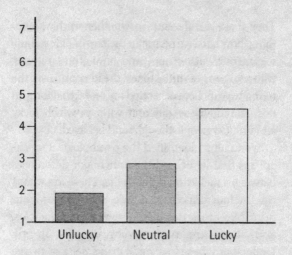

Unlucky, neutral, and lucky people's confidence of winning the lottery

dent and 7 indicated that they were extremely confident. When my colleagues and I went back and analyzed the results we discovered something surprising. As shown in the above graph, *lucky people's expectations of winning were more than twice that of unlucky people.*[7]

When it comes to random events like the lottery, such expectations count for little. Someone with a high expectation of winning will do as well as someone with a low expectation. But life is not like a lottery. Often, our expectations make a difference.

They make a difference in whether we try something, how hard we persist in the face of failure, how we interact with others, and how others interact with us. It was essential to test the idea, and over the next few years I concentrated my research efforts on understanding the different ways in which lucky and unlucky people thought and behaved.

Eventually, I identified the psychological mechanisms that lie behind the four major differences between a lucky and unlucky life. These are what I call the four principles of luck. Each of these four principles break down into several subprinciples, and there are twelve subprinciples in all. Understand these four main principles and twelve subprinciples, and you understand luck itself.

The following four chapters outline these principles and subprinciples in detail. They discuss the many different kinds of research that I conducted to discover the principles and the impact that they have upon the lives of lucky and unlucky people. I have included many real-life examples from the people who were kind enough to participate in my work, and there are various opportunities here for you to evaluate the role of these principles in your life. At the end of each chapter I outline various exercises that will help increase the amount of luck that you experience in your life.

It is time to begin—time to start to uncover the real secrets behind a lucky life.

Section Two

The Four Principles of Luck

CHAPTER THREE

Principle One: Maximize Your Chance Opportunities

**Principle:
Lucky people create, notice,
and act upon the chance
opportunities in their lives.**

Lucky people's lives are full of chance opportu-nities. In the last chapter I described the life of professional poet Jodie, whose lucky chance encounters have helped her achieve many of her lifelong dreams and ambitions. We also met Lee, a marketing manager who has an uncanny knack for being in the right place at the right time. He met his future wife by chance and puts much of his success in business down to lucky encounters. And then there was serial competition winner Lynne. The entire course of Lynne's life was altered when, quite by chance, she came across a newspaper article about a woman who had won several prizes in competitions. Lynne, Lee, and Jodie are typical of the lucky people involved in my research. Without their trying, opportunities just seem to come their way.

Lucky people are often convinced that these opportunities are the result of pure chance. They just happen to open newspapers at the right place, come across the right site on the Internet, walk down the street at the right time, or go to a party and meet the right person. But my work revealed that these seemingly chance opportunities are the result of lucky people's psychological makeup. The way they think and behave makes them far more likely than others to create, notice, and act upon chance opportunities in their lives. I uncovered hitherto unexplored techniques that lucky people use to maximize the role of seemingly chance opportunities in their lives. I discovered that being in the right place at the right time is actually all about being in the right state of mind.

Wendy is a forty-year-old housewife. She considers herself lucky in many aspects of her life but is especially fortunate when it comes to winning competitions. On average, she wins about three prizes a week. Some of these prizes are quite small, but many have been substantial. In the last five years she has won large cash prizes and several major vacations abroad. Wendy certainly seems to have a magical ability to win competitions. And she is not the only one. In the previous chapter I described how Lynne has won several large prizes in competitions, including several cars and trips. The same was also true of Joe. Like both Wendy and Lynne, Joe considers himself to be very lucky in many areas of his life. He has been happily married for forty years and has a loving family. But Joe is especially lucky in competitions, and his recent list of successes has included winning televisions, a day spent on the set of a well-known television soap opera, and several vacations.

What is behind Lynne, Wendy, and Joe's winning ways? Their secret is surprisingly simple. They all enter a very large number of competitions. Each week, Wendy enters about sixty postal competitions and about seventy Internet-based competitions. Likewise, both Lynne and Joe enter about fifty competitions a week. And their chances of winning are increased with each and every entry. All three of them are well aware that their lucky winning ways are, in reality, due to the large number of competitions they enter. As Wendy explained, "I am a lucky person, but luck is what you make it. I win a lot of competitions and prizes. But I do put a huge amount of effort into it." And Joe commented:

> People always said to me they think I'm very lucky because of the amount of competitions that I win. But then they tell me that they don't enter many themselves, and I think, "Well, if you don't enter, you have no chance of winning." They look at me as being very lucky, but I think you make your own luck . . . as I say to them, "You've got to be in to win."

I wondered whether the same idea might also account for the other types of opportunities that lucky people constantly encounter in their lives. Could this explain why they often meet interesting people at parties and come across newspaper articles that change their lives? I managed to go backstage and discover the reality behind the illusion. And my research revealed that it could all be summed up in just one word—personality.

People who tend to think and behave in the same way are said to have the same personality. The concept of personality is central to modern-day psychology, and a huge amount of time and effort has been invested in working out the best way of accurately classifying personalities. Although it has often been far from easy, the results have been very impressive.

For many years, psychologists have tried to develop accurate ways of classifying people on the basis of their personality. After years of research, most now agree that there are only five underlying dimensions to our personalities— five dimensions on which we all vary. These dimensions have been found in both the young and old, in men and women, and across many different cultures. These dimensions are often referred to as *agreeableness, conscientiousness, extroversion, neuroticism, and openness.*[1]

I compared the personalities of lucky and unlucky people on the five dimensions of personality. The first dimension I examined was agreeableness. This is a measure of the degree to which someone is sympathetic toward others and willing to help them. I wondered whether lucky people were the recipients of large amounts of good fortune because they tended to help others, and so others tended to help them in return. Interestingly, lucky people scored no higher on agreeableness than unlucky people.

The second dimension I examined was that of conscientiousness. This is a measure of the degree to which a person is self-disciplined, strong-willed, and determined. Perhaps lucky people experienced more good fortune because they simply worked harder than unlucky people. But once again, there was very little difference in the conscientiousness scores of lucky and unlucky people.[2]

The groups did, however, obtain very different scores on the remaining three personality dimensions—extroversion, neuroticism, and openness. The differences explained why lucky people constantly encounter chance opportunities in their lives while unlucky people do not. Each of these personality traits relates to a different subprinciple that follows.

Subprinciple 1:
Lucky people build and maintain
a strong "network of luck."

My research revealed that lucky people scored much higher than unlucky people on a dimension of personality known as extroversion.[3] Extroverts are far more sociable than introverts. They enjoy spending time visiting friends and going to parties, and tend to be attracted to jobs that involve working with other people. Introverts are far more inward-looking. They are happy to spend time on their own and feel most contented when engaged in more solitary activities, such as reading a good book.

Additional research revealed that there are three ways in which lucky people's extroversion significantly increases the likelihood of their having a lucky chance encounter—meeting a large number of people, being a "social magnet," and keeping in contact with people.

First, in the same way that Lynne, Joe, and Wendy increase their chances of winning prizes by entering many competitions, so lucky people dramatically increase the possibility of a lucky chance encounter by meeting a large number of people in their daily lives. The concept is simple. The more people they meet, the greater opportunity they have of running into someone who could have a positive effect on their lives.

Take the case of Robert, a forty-five-year-old aircraft safety officer from England. Robert is very lucky and his life is peppered with chance encounters. A few years ago, Robert and his wife flew to France to celebrate the New Year. They had intended to fly back a few days later, but heavy snowfall grounded all available flights. As the snow wasn't going to clear for days, Robert and his wife decided to return to England by ferry, and made their way to the French port of Boulogne. But there was a problem; the ferry was going to arrive at a port that was a considerable distance from their house, and the heavy snowfall had so disrupted public transportation that it was going to be impossible for them to make their way home from the port. Just as Robert and his wife were discussing the problem, the door of the waiting room opened and in walked another British

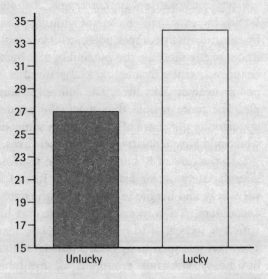

Extroversion scores of unlucky and lucky people

couple who were also going to catch the ferry. Robert started to chat with them, and was amazed to discover that they lived very close to his home. The couple offered to give Robert and his wife a lift home from the port.

Another time, Robert and his wife wanted to move. They had looked at several houses but not seen anything they liked. One day, Robert just happened to be out walking and saw a real estate agent he knew coming out of his office. Robert could have kept walking but instead decided to ask the agent whether he had any suitable properties available. The agent said that he was sorry but he didn't, and started to walk away. A few seconds later he turned around and suggested that Robert look at a house that had only just come on the market. Robert immediately drove around to the house, fell in love with it, and bought it that day. Robert and his wife have been living there for more than twenty years and describe it as their dream house.

When I interviewed him, Robert described himself as very outgoing and talkative. He told me that if he is standing in a supermarket line, he will often start chatting to the people next to him, and described how he frequently strikes up conversations with strangers. Robert really enjoys meeting people and spending time with them.

And the more people he meets, the greater his chances of coming into contact with someone who can have a beneficial effect on his life.

Joseph, a thirty-five-year-old mature student, has also encountered life-changing chance opportunities in his life. When he was young he found it very difficult to settle down in school and was in constant trouble with the police. By his late twenties he had drifted in and out of prison for several minor offenses, and from one job to another. Then a chance encounter changed his life. He was traveling on a train in Virginia when it became stuck between two stations. Joseph became bored and struck up a conversation with the woman sitting next to him. She was a psychologist, and the two of them started to talk about Joseph's life, and he began to confess to some of his self-destructive tendencies. The woman was impressed with his insight and social skills, and suggested that he would make an excellent psychologist. As the train pulled into the station the two of them parted company, but the woman's idea stuck in Joseph's mind. He looked into the type of training and qualifications he would need to become a psychologist. He eventually made the decision to change his entire lifestyle and go to college. He is currently studying psychology at a southern university and will graduate next year. Joseph told me: "I've just learned that if you initiate conversation with people you can get a lot out of it—to me, it improves my luck immensely."

Many other lucky people also reported how they consistently experienced good luck by simply connecting with the people they met on a daily basis. Take the case of Samantha. A few years ago she was working as a young secretary in a legal firm, secretly hoping to expand her horizons and get a job in the film world. The only problem was that she had no contacts and no rich relations to help her. On a rainy afternoon she walked out of a doctor's appointment and hailed a cab on Central Park West in New York City to get back to her office. Just as the cab arrived, an older man walked up to her and asked if he could share the car with her. Samantha was naturally outgoing, and as they rode through the park, she struck up a conversation with him and discovered that he was an executive at a movie company. She told him of her secret longings to be part of the film world and how she would be glad to accept the lowliest of jobs to gain an entrée. He arranged for her to meet with the personnel director at his company and she was immediately offered a starting position as a secretary to a lawyer. She soon made the transition to film acquisitions.

Five years later Samantha is a busy, successful film executive in Los Angeles who recognizes that she seized an opportunity while being in the right place at the right time.

Another way in which lucky people increase the likelihood of chance encounters in their lives revolves around a concept known as "social magnetism." Psychologists have noticed that certain people seem able to draw other people toward them.[4] These social magnets often find that whenever they go to parties or attend meetings, strangers initiate conversations with them. When they walk along the street, people frequently ask them for directions or the correct time. For some strange reason, other people just seem drawn to them. And, perhaps not surprisingly, far more extroverts than introverts are social magnets.

Research has revealed that these people attract others because, without realizing it, social magnets exhibit the types of body language and facial expressions that other people find attractive and inviting. And interestingly, lucky people exhibit exactly the same pattern of behaviors. I asked some fellow psychologists to watch the videotapes of interviews that I had conducted with lucky and unlucky people. I removed the soundtrack from the interviews so that the people had no way of knowing which of the interviewees were lucky and which were unlucky. I asked everyone to rate how my interviewees looked and behaved during the interviews. They counted the number of times they smiled, measured the amount of eye contact they made, and noted whether they used certain gestures.

The differences between the lucky and unlucky people were dramatic. The lucky people smiled twice as much as the unlucky people and engaged in far more eye contact. But perhaps the biggest differences emerged when we examined the degree to which they engaged in "open" or "closed" body language. People exhibit "closed" body language when they cross their arms and legs and orient themselves away from the person they are speaking to. "Open" body language is exactly the opposite. People point their bodies toward the person that they are speaking to, uncross their arms and legs, and often make gestures that involve them displaying open palms. Lucky people tended to engage in three times as much open body language as unlucky people.

Lucky people's body language and facial expressions attract other people to them. And, again, the more people they meet, the greater the probability of their having a chance encounter. The more people they talk to at a party, the greater their chances of meeting their dream partner. The more people they talk to about business, the greater their chances of meeting a new client or someone who can have a beneficial impact on their career.

Still, this wasn't the full picture. In addition to initiating conversations with lots of people and being social magnets, lucky extroverts also engage in a third type of behavior that increases the probability of living a life full of chance opportunities. And this third type of behavior plays perhaps the biggest role in their success.

Lucky people are effective at building secure, and long-lasting, attachments with the people they meet. They are easy to get to know and most people like them.

> "Luck is believing you're lucky."
> —TENNESSEE WILLIAMS

They tend to be trusting and form close friendships with others. As a result, they often keep in touch with a much larger number of friends and colleagues than unlucky people. And time and time again, this network of friends helps promote opportunity in their lives.

Take the case of Kathy, a fifty-year-old administrator from Syracuse, New York. Kathy considers herself to be extremely lucky in all areas of her life. She has been happily married for twenty-three years and has two healthy children. She described herself as always being in the right place at the right time. A few years ago she was considering returning to work after having taken a career break to bring up her children. She wasn't sure if her skills were still marketable. She called an old friend in the business world and arranged to meet him. She sought his advice for reentry, and as they started to chat about his new promotion, he mentioned that he was going to advertise for a personal assistant very soon. Kathy said that she would be willing to start again at that position and he suggested that she apply. Kathy was offered the job and accepted. Six years later she is still working at the same company and loves the job. Kathy told me that she puts much of her luck down to her attitude toward people:

I'm a collector of people, I like people and don't have any problems making friends. And I try to keep in touch with them all. You can't keep in touch with everybody, but I try my best.

Kathy has built up an impressive network of friends and colleagues dating back to elementary school and high school. To celebrate her birthday, she organized a dinner for her fifty closest friends. She had kept in touch with people from all parts of the world and from all stages of her life—people she had met in her childbirth classes and in her early days as a working mother.

Kathy wasn't the only lucky person to stress the importance of keeping in touch with friends and colleagues. In the previous chapter we met Jodie, a professional poet now living in New York. For the past two years she has been very lucky, and chance encounters have helped her to achieve many of her lifelong dreams and ambitions. Jodie increases the likelihood of such chance encounters in her life by engaging in conversation with people that she meets and keeping in touch with them. She is also well connected within her community of writers and poets and knows hundreds of people on a first-name basis. I asked her about this aspect of her life:

> When I interact with people, it's completely sincere and authentic, and I really care about the relationships. I don't feel like a writer holed up in my house. Our communities are homes. So when I realized who my communities are— who's really supporting me, where I feel

like I'm in a family—I got very busy nur-
turing those communities, and trying to
figure out how to stay in touch with
them.

These techniques are often especially effective because they help set up, and maintain, a
huge "network of luck." Sociologists have estimated that on average we all know approxi-
mately 300 people on a first-name basis. When
we meet someone and start talking to them, we
are only one step, or handshake, away from the
people that they know. Let's suppose that you
are at a party and start talking to a woman
named Sue. You have never met Sue before, but
she seems friendly and you mention that you
are thinking of changing jobs. It is unlikely that
Sue would be in a position to hire you, but she
might know someone who is. By talking to Sue,
you are only a handshake away from the 300
people that she knows on a first-name basis.
But it doesn't end there. Each of Sue's friends
also knows 300 people on first-name terms.
Sue might introduce you to someone who is
likely to know someone else interested in hiring you. You are only two handshakes away
from roughly 300 x 300 people—90,000 new
possibilities for a chance opportunity, just by
saying hello to Sue.

Let's return to Kathy's fiftieth birthday party and her fifty guests from all parts of her life. Let's assume that each of these fifty people knew, on average, 300 different people on first-name basis, and that each of them also knew another 300 people. Sitting at her birthday table, Kathy was just one handshake away from 15,000 people and two handshakes away from 4.5 million people! Given all of these potential contacts, it is perhaps not surprising that chance opportunities play such an important and positive role in Kathy's life.

Without realizing it, lucky people behave in a way that maximizes the chance opportunities in their lives. They talk to lots of people and spend time with them, attract other people to them and keep in touch with people. These actions result in a massive "network of luck" and a huge potential for chance opportunities. And it takes only one chance encounter to change a life.

Building a "Network of Luck"

Jessica is a forensic scientist from Chicago and has been lucky throughout her entire life:

> I have my dream job, two wonderful children, and a great guy that I love very much. It's amazing, but when I look back at my life I realize that I have been lucky in just absolutely every area. Academic, friendships, meeting certain people, being in the right place at the right time, I can't think of a single area where I've been unlucky.

Jessica has been especially lucky in her love life. She has always found it easy to meet partners and form lasting relationships with them. She is currently in a seven-year relationship with a man that she considers to be "perfect." In one interview, I asked her to describe how she had met her present partner.

> I met him completely by chance

at a dinner party. One night, a friend unexpectedly called me and asked if I would like to go to a dinner party with her. I hadn't intended to go out that night, but thought that it sounded like fun. We went along, and that's where I met the love of my life. He had also been dragged along by a friend of his.

I asked Jessica to explain what was behind her luck:

A large part of it stems from just being out there. If you're busy and active, you meet lots of people and enter other spheres. I tend to chat with strangers and I think it's that aspect of my personality that has brought me many of my friends and lovers. I'll seek out interesting people rather than be bored. If I go to an event or a party, I'll try and make certain that I find somebody that's interesting to talk to. Friends have told me that people are drawn to me because I am interested in them. I don't just talk to people, I listen to them as well. It's about sharing information. And I go to quite a lot of effort to connect with other people.

I also hold lots of parties. People generally say things like, "Oh, that was a great party, you have such wonderful parties." I tend to invite lots of different people. Parties with the same people get a little too predictable. And it's a great way to introduce people to other people, and bring new people into the fold. I hold them every couple of months. And it really promotes my luck, in terms of careers and assistance, the little bits of tips we get in terms of financial planning and so on—it's about sharing expertise and experiences.

It's a probability game. If you meet twenty people in a week, chances are you're gonna meet someone who's interesting. So, part of it's just improving your odds of experiencing nice events, nice encounters, by being out there. I think it'd be pretty hard to be lucky if you weren't.

Subprinciple 2:
Lucky people have a relaxed
attitude toward life.

There is also another set of techniques that
lucky people unconsciously use to their advantage. These techniques are not so much concerned with the creation of chance opportunities but instead enhance lucky people's ability to
notice and act upon opportunities that arise
naturally. This basic idea can be illustrated with
a simple card trick. Imagine that I've invited
some guests to dinner. I've placed five playing
cards face up on the table. I ask one guest to
look at the cards, choose one, and remember it.

Next, I ask the guest to leave the room for a few
minutes. I pick up the cards, look at each of them,
and decide which one I think the guest chose. I
take that card and put it in my pocket and put
four cards back on the table. I invite the guest
back into the room and ask him to look at the
cards and tell me if his card is missing. I have performed this many times and am always correct.

I thought it might be fun to try it now.
Performing a card trick in a book isn't easy, but let's
give it a go. I have reproduced five cards below.
Look at them, choose one, and remember it.

Got one? Good. Now, imagine that you have

left the room and I have pocketed my prediction. I invite you back into the room and show you the four cards on the table. My prediction is that your card will be missing. The four cards are in Appendix A, on page 349. Go and see if your card is missing.

How did I do? Was your card there? I have to come clean with you. As you might have already worked out, this has nothing to do with my amazing magical abilities. It does, however, have everything to do with psychology.

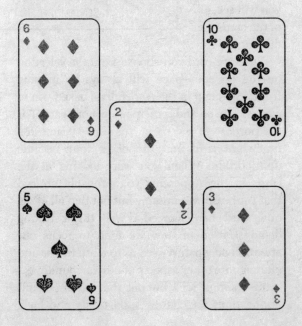

This trick works because of a very simple psychological principle, namely, that we only tend to notice only those things that are important to us. If you haven't already worked out the secret behind the trick, have a second look at the cards printed on the previous page. Instead of choosing just one card, make a note of all of them. Now turn to Appendix A and look at the cards there. As you will see, all of the cards are different.

> "Diligence is the mother of good luck."
> —BENJAMIN FRANKLIN

Whatever card you choose from the selection on the previous page will always be missing from the lineup in the Appendix. I asked you to concentrate on and remember just one card. For the purpose of the trick, this card became the important card and the other four became unimportant. When you were looking at the cards in the Appendix, you probably noticed that your card was missing but not that all of the other cards had changed as well. It is a striking demonstration of how we tend to focus our attention on whatever seems to matter to us and often ignore other aspects of our surroundings.

It is a simple idea, but one that has important implications for chance opportunity and luck.

Quite often, we are simply unaware of the opportunities that surround us because we are too focused on looking for something else.

I carried out a very simple experiment into the phenomenon. I gave people a newspaper and asked them to look through it and tell me how many photographs were inside. It all seemed fair and aboveboard. I simply wanted to know how many photographs were in the newspaper. Everyone found the task very easy, and it took most of them about two minutes to look through the newspaper and count the photographs. A few people took slightly longer because they went through the newspaper a second time and double-checked.

In fact, all of them could have told me the answer within seconds, and without going to the bother of counting the photographs. Why? Because the second page of the newspaper contained a message that said, STOP COUNTING—THERE ARE 43 PHOTOGRAPHS IN THIS NEWSPAPER. This was not a small message tucked away in the corner of the page. This message took up half of the page and was written in type that was over one-and-a-half inches high. It was a huge message, staring everyone straight in the face. But nobody saw it because everyone was too focused on looking for photographs.

They also missed out on something far more

important; namely, an opportunity to win $250. Halfway through the newspaper I placed a second, huge message. Again, this one took up half of the page and announced, in huge type, STOP COUNTING, TELL THE EXPERIMENTER YOU HAVE SEEN THIS AND WIN $250. Again, every single person missed the message. They were all too busy looking for the photographs. It was interesting to watch their behavior at the end of the experiment. I asked them if they had seen anything unusual in the newspaper. When they said that they hadn't, I asked them to just flip through the newspaper a second time. Within seconds they saw the first message. Many of the people laughed out loud and said they were very surprised that they had missed it. When they saw the second message, they were even more amazed, and their language was significantly more colorful.

All the people who took part in the experiment failed to notice important and obvious opportunities because they weren't looking out for them.

The important question is what sorts of people do notice these types of opportunities? Who spots that all the cards have changed in the magic trick? Who sees the opportunity to win $250 in the newspaper experiment? The answer lies in a second major dimension of personality on which lucky and unlucky people differ—neuroticism. People who obtain a low score on this dimension are generally calm and relaxed, while people who obtain a high score are more tense and anxious.

As shown in the following graph, lucky people have much lower neuroticism scores on the personality test than unlucky people.[5] And this can make a big difference when it comes to their being relaxed enough to notice chance opportunities.

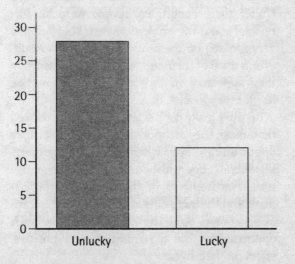

Neuroticism scores of unlucky and lucky people

Psychologists have conducted many studies into the effects that anxiety has on our ability to notice something that we aren't looking for. In one well-known experiment, people were asked to watch carefully a moving dot in the center of a computer screen. Without warning, the experimenters would occasionally flash large dots at the edges of the computer screen. Nearly all of the participants noticed these large dots. The psychologists then carried out the same experiment with a second group of people, but this time they offered them a large financial reward for accurately watching the center dot. Under these conditions, people were far less relaxed about the whole situation. They became very focused on the center dot and, as a result, over a third of them missed the large dots when they appeared on the computer screen. The harder they looked, the less they saw.

Because lucky people tend to be more relaxed than most, they are more likely to notice chance opportunities, even when they are not expecting them. They will be the people who notice the advertisements in the newspaper experiment and the large dots at the edges of the computer screen. And the ability to notice such opportunities has a significant, and positive, effect on their lives.

To illustrate the point, let's start by discussing

how this factor can influence a very simple aspect of luck, namely, whether you tend to find money in the street. As Huckleberry Finn remarked, we take more pleasure in the dollar that we find on the street than the dollar we earn. Richard, age sixty-seven, often comes across coins, and even bills, on sidewalks. Eight years ago he decided to put the money aside in a special jug marked "found money." He keeps the jug in his kitchen and is amazed at how quickly it fills up. In one interview, Richard described how he had noticed a rather strange phenomenon—the amount of money he found seemed to be directly related to how happy he felt. Richard had noticed this because, for a while, he had kept a note of the relationship between the amount of "found" money he came across on the street and whether he felt relaxed and happy or anxious and sad. His findings demonstrated the important role that these factors played in his noticing the opportunities that surrounded him:

I didn't tend to find money when I was feeling a bit low or thinking, "Oh, I can't be bothered today." If I was in a happy, relaxed mood, striding out along the road, I was much more likely to find it because my senses seemed more acute and more aware. It's odd. I don't actually go out looking for money, but because I'm not thinking about anything in particular, I seem much more likely to find it.

Lucky people's ability to notice opportunities is a result of their relaxed way of looking at the world. It is not that they expect to find certain opportunities, but rather that they notice them when they come across them. In contrast, unlucky people tend to be more anxious. They are the type of people who are so busy counting the photographs in the newspaper that they don't notice the advertisement offering them an opportunity to win $250 instantly. In real life, they might be focused on getting to a meeting on time, thinking about finding a new job, or worrying about the problems in their lives. As a result, they have a very narrow, focused beam of attention that can cause them to miss the unexpected opportunities that surround them on a daily basis.

The lucky people in my study often remarked upon how they had come across life-changing opportunities in newspapers and magazines and on bulletin boards and the Internet. In Chapter Two I described the lucky life of Lynne. Her entire life changed when she chanced across a newspaper article about a woman who had won lots of prizes in competitions. Many other lucky people reported similar experiences. Take the case of Diana, a thirty-nine-year-old professor of education from Cambridge University. She told me how one very important episode in her life came about through a newspaper article that just happened to catch her eye:

> Something that made a major impact on my life was when I read about someone talking about the problems surrounding preschool education in Britain. I wrote back and said I couldn't agree more. The writer invited me to come and meet him, and it turned out that he had a connection to a government advisory committee on education, and because I impressed them I wound up running part of the government's program for preschool education.

Other lucky people spoke about how they would come across chance opportunities on television or the radio. Elizabeth, a sixty-two-year-old yoga coach in Boston, puts much of her good luck down to her "magic radio," which always presents her with wonderful opportunities:

> I switch on my "magic radio" and more

times than is conceivable by chance, it has an item on it that is exactly what I need. A while ago I was going through a divorce and my lawyer said that I needed a private detective. The next day, a local radio program had an interview with the head of an association of private detectives. So I called him and he recommended a private detective who lived near me. I got in touch with the man and hired him—he turned out to be really good. And on another occasion I wanted to broaden my outlook on life, turned on the radio, and heard a woman talking about this fascinating sociology class at a local college. So I called the radio station, found out some details, and a few weeks later was enrolled in a weeklong residential course in sociology on a beautiful campus. My magic radio does a lot of that.

But being relaxed does not just help lucky people notice money in the street, or spot helpful items in newspapers and magazines and hear them on the radio. Exactly the same principle applies when they meet and chat with other people. They do not go to parties and meetings trying hard to find their dream partners or someone who will offer them their perfect job. Instead, they are simply relaxed and therefore more attuned to the opportunities around them. They go to parties and listen to people. Lucky people see what is there, rather than trying to find what they want to see. As a result, they are far more receptive to any opportunities that arise naturally.

John, a lucky accountant from Nevada, commented on how he had come across many positive opportunities by relaxing and not being so rigid in what he was looking for:

I think that part of my luck is because I am more relaxed and open to whatever's out there, rather than looking for real specific things. A little while ago, I wanted a really good car—a recent model with low mileage. Now, if I would have thought, "I want a used Mercedes, at so much mileage, and whatever," I probably wouldn't have found it. But I just relaxed and left it open. I found a great car by looking in the classifieds—it's not a Mercedes, but it's perfect for me. And, when I moved to Las Vegas in February, I looked at two houses and I managed to find the perfect place. If I had put too many specifications on it, I wouldn't have found the right thing. But I was more relaxed and so instantly spotted

a great house. So what I've found is that if
I want a very specific thing, then life's not
so lucky. But if I relax and leave it open,
everything always turns out much better.

In short, lucky people are skilled at spotting
any opportunities that naturally arise. They are
not actively looking for these opportunities, but
their relaxed approach to life helps them notice
what is happening around them. It is rather
ironic, but by not trying too hard to look, they
end up seeing far more.

YOUR LUCK JOURNAL: EXERCISE 5

What Chance Opportunities
Have You Missed in Your Life?

Think back to a recent situation where
you missed an opportunity to talk with
someone that you didn't know very well
and would have liked to have gotten to
know better. Perhaps you saw someone at
a party who appeared especially attractive
or friendly, but you felt too shy to make
the first move. Or maybe you heard some-

one give a fascinating talk but then didn't have a chance to chat with the speaker. Perhaps you attended a soirée at work, saw someone that you had heard a great deal about, but that person left just before you could introduce yourself. Possibly someone caught your eye in a store but it didn't seem an appropriate time or place to initiate a conversation. Or a friend or colleague may have introduced you to someone she knew, but you were in a hurry and you didn't really have time to get to know that person.

Take a few moments to close your eyes and replay the event in your mind. Think of the way the person was dressed, the way he or she behaved and the reason you missed the opportunity to get to know the person. Jot down a brief description of these details in your Luck Journal.

Now I want you to turn back the clock and imagine that a completely different set of events took place. Imagine yourself in a parallel universe where anything and everything is possible. In this new world you actually met the person and had an opportunity to chat with them. Perhaps you found the courage to say hello to the person at the party. Or maybe you bumped into the speaker on the stairwell after his fascinating talk. You and the person could have reached for the same item at exactly the same time in the store and started chatting. Perhaps you managed to introduce yourself to the person before she left the soirée after work. Or maybe you weren't in such a hurry when your friend introduced you to the person and so the three of you had time to go for coffee. In your Luck Journal, note down a few details about how the two of you met.

Next, imagine that you found the person approachable and very easy to talk to. In fact, imagine that the meeting went so well that it had an extraordinarily positive effect on your life. Perhaps the person at the party turned out to be your perfect partner and the two of you fell deeply in love. Maybe the meeting in the stairwell resulted in an amazing career opportunity. Or the person in the store may have become one of your closest friends. Perhaps the conversation at the work soirée resulted in an incredible business deal. Let your imagination run wild as you think about how the chance meeting changed your life. Now, jot down a brief description of the transformational effect of the meeting in your Luck Journal.

This exercise is designed to illustrate the power of chance opportunities—how the smallest of events and decisions can have a huge impact on your life. In reality, we obviously cannot turn back the clock and change the past. There is simply no way of knowing what would have happened if you had actually met that mystery person. It is possible, however, to change your future. There are various techniques that will greatly increase the likelihood that you will actually experience the type of chance encounter you have just described in your Luck Journal. And the first step toward incorporating these techniques into your life is to have a thorough understanding of the simple, but highly effective, theories that lie behind them.

Subprinciple 3:
Lucky people are open to
new experiences in their lives.

There is a third and final set of unexplored techniques that lucky people unconsciously use to promote the good fortune they encounter. And these techniques center around another important dimension of their personalities, "openness." People who obtain a high score on this dimension like to have a great deal of variety and novelty in their lives. They love trying new experiences, new kinds of foods and new ways of doing things. They don't tend to be bound by convention and they like the notion of unpredictability. People who obtain a low score on openness tend to be much more conventional. They tend to like to do things the way that they have been done in the past. They like the idea of tomorrow being broadly similar to yesterday and today. And they don't enjoy big surprises.

As shown in the following graph, lucky people have much higher openness scores on the personality test than unlucky people.6 And this greater openness can help promote the chance opportunities in their lives.

At the start of this chapter we met Robert, our lucky aircraft safety engineer whose chance meetings always paid off. In one interview, Robert emphasized his preference for variety in his life: "When it comes to vacations, we never book in advance, we just fly on the spur of the moment and get a hotel when we get there."

Eugenie is a thirty-two-year-old housewife. Eugenie's whole life is driven by the need for new experiences. She has worked in many different types of jobs and never been on vacation to the

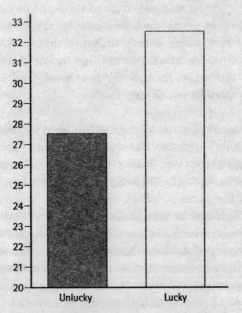

Openness scores of unlucky and lucky people

same destination twice. She is a member of a local craft club. Whereas most other members stick to the same craft, Eugenie has tried everything, from ceramics to sewing, china painting to curtain making. She is also always trying out new products and her house is full of different kinds of breakfast cereals, washing powders, deodorants, and toothpastes. As she explained to me, the principle even affects her weekly trips to surrounding stores:

> If you told me to go to the same store every single week and pick up the same thirty items, exactly the same, that would drive me mad. I have to go to one store one week, another the next week, and a third the week after that.

Many of my lucky participants went to considerable lengths to introduce variety and change into their lives. Before making an important decision, one lucky participant would make a list of the various options and roll dice to decide which one he should actually choose. Another person described a special technique that he had developed to force himself to meet different types of people. He had noticed that whenever he went to a party, he tended to talk to the same type of people. To help disrupt this routine and make life more fun, he thinks of a color before he arrives at a party and then chooses to speak only to people wearing that color at the party! At some parties he spoke only to women in red, at another he chatted exclusively to men in black.

Although it may seem strange, under certain circumstances, this type of behavior will actually increase the number of chance opportunities in our lives. Imagine living in the center of a large apple orchard. Each day you have to venture into the orchard and collect a large basket of apples. The first few times it won't matter where you decide to visit. All parts of the orchard will have apples and so you will be able to find them wherever you go. But as time goes on it will become more and more difficult to find apples in the places that you have visited before. And the more you return to the same locations, the harder it will be to find apples there. But if you decide to always go to parts of the orchard that you have never visited before, or even randomly decide where to go, your chances of finding apples will be greatly increased.

It is exactly the same with luck. It is easy to exhaust the opportunities in your life. Keep on talking to the same people in the same way. Keep taking the same route to and from work. Keep going to the same places on vacation. But new or even random experiences introduce the potential for new opportunities. It is like visiting

a new part of the orchard. Suddenly you are surrounded by hundreds of apples.

Same Opportunities, Different Lives

During my research I spoke to countless lucky
and unlucky people. But my two most unusual
interviews were with unlucky Brenda and lucky
Martin. Brenda is accident prone. A few years ago
she tripped over her dog and fell onto the corner of
a sofa. The following day she developed a pain in
her side. The pain slowly grew worse and she started to experience serious breathing problems. A
visit to her local doctor revealed that the small
knock on the soft sofa had resulted in a collapsed
lung. This sort of event is not at all uncommon in
Brenda's life. Brenda considered herself to be very
unlucky and was, in her own words, "a walking disaster." Martin was quite different. A few years ago,
he bought a ticket for the UK National Lottery.
That evening he was lying in the bath listening to
the result of the draw on television. When his first
three numbers were announced, Martin jumped
out of the bath and ran into the living room.
Martin couldn't believe his luck as his fourth, fifth,
and sixth numbers all came up. Martin won a jack-
pot prize of over £7 million and, perhaps not surprisingly, considers himself a very lucky man.

At the start of their interviews I asked Brenda

and Martin to tell me about any lucky or unlucky events that had happened to them recently. I have asked many lucky and unlucky people this question over the years. This time the situation was different. This time, I already knew the answers. In fact, I knew more about the recent events in Brenda and Martin's lives than they did. Although they didn't realize it, they had been taking part in an experiment to examine the relationship between luck and chance opportunities.

Unlike most of my work, this experiment hadn't happened in a university laboratory but had instead taken place during Brenda and Martin's everyday lives. Not only that, we had filmed the whole thing. This footage, and the comments made by Brenda and Martin during their interviews, revealed some telling insights into why lucky people experience far more chance opportunities in their lives than unlucky people.

A few weeks before, I had met up with a television producer making a program about my research into luck. She said that several lucky and unlucky people—including Martin and Brenda—had volunteered to take part in the program, and were eager to participate in some experiments. I wanted to illustrate how lucky people created the chance opportunities in their lives by presenting Martin and Brenda with exactly the same opportunities and seeing how each of them reacted. But I didn't want to do it in the laboratory. I wanted to do it in the real world.

Although the idea was simple, it required a large amount of planning, a supply of £5 notes, four decoys, and lots of cameras. The experiment took place in a coffee shop close to my university. The television crew rigged up several cameras along the street leading up to the coffee shop and throughout the coffee shop itself. We asked Martin and Brenda to go to the coffee shop at different times and wait there until they were met by someone involved with our research.

We created two potential "chance" opportunities for both Martin and Brenda. We placed a crisp £5 note on the pavement directly outside the coffee shop. Martin and Brenda would have to walk past it to enter the shop—but would they notice the money? We also rearranged the coffee shop so that it contained only four tables, and we placed a decoy at each of the tables. One of them was a successful businessman, the others were not. All four people were instructed to behave in exactly the same way, regardless of whether it was Brenda or Martin in the coffee shop. Would Brenda and Martin make the most of the opportunity?

We set the cameras rolling and waited for Martin and Brenda to arrive. Martin was first to arrive at the coffee shop. He immediately noticed the £5 note, picked it up, and walked into the shop. Once inside, he ordered a coffee and sat down next to the successful business-man. Within minutes, Martin had introduced himself and offered to buy the man a coffee. The man accepted, and a few moments later the two of them were chatting away. After Martin left the shop we placed another £5 note on the ground and waited for Brenda.

Then things went slightly wrong. Instead of Brenda, a woman pushing a stroller walked up the street. She noticed the money, picked it up, and walked off. I suspect that she is a consistently lucky person but I will never know for sure. We placed another £5 note on the ground and waited. A few minutes later, Brenda appeared. She walked straight over the note and into the coffee shop. She went up to the counter, ordered a coffee, and sat down next to the businessman. Unlike Martin, she sat there quietly and didn't say a word to anyone.

In the afternoon, I interviewed both of them about any lucky and unlucky events that had happened to them that day. Brenda looked at me blankly and said that it had been an uneventful morning. Martin gave a colorful description of how he had found £5 on the street and had a very enjoyable chat with a businessman in a coffee shop.

Same opportunities. Different lives.

YOUR LUCK JOURNAL: EXERCISE 6

Your Luck Profile: Principle One

Let's return to your scores on the Luck Profile from page xix. The first three items on that questionnaire relate to the subprinciples discussed in this chapter. Item 1 is a simple measure of your extroversion, Item 2 concerns how anxious you tend to be and Item 3 relates to your level of openness to new experiences.

Scoring:

Look back at the ratings you assigned to these three items and then add up those numbers to create a single score (see the following example). This is your score for the first principle of luck.

Statement	Your rating (1–5)
1 I sometimes chat with strangers when standing in a supermarket or bank line.	5
2 I do not have a tendency to	4

worry and feel anxious about life.

3   I am open to new experiences,   3
    such as trying new types of food
    or drinks.

Total for the first principle of luck   12

Now look at the following scale to discover whether your score would be categorized as high, medium, or low. Please make a note of your score and category in your Luck Journal, as these results will become important when we come to discuss how best to enhance the luck in your life.

Low   Medium   High

3 4 5 6 7 8 • 9 10 11 • 12 13 14 15
⬠

I have asked a large number of lucky, unlucky, and neutral people to complete the Luck Profile. Lucky people tend to score much higher on these items than other people. Unlucky people tend to obtain the lowest scores (see the following graph).

Summary

Lucky people are more likely than unlucky people to create, notice, and act upon chance opportunities. They do this in various ways. They initiate conversations with more people because they are extroverts. More people start to talk to them because of their social magnetism. And they are good at keeping in touch with people. Lucky people are also more relaxed than unlucky people, and this makes them more able to notice unexpected chance opportunities in many different aspects of their lives. Finally, lucky people also introduce more variety and new experiences into their lives, which helps to increase the likelihood of their experiencing, and maximizing, chance opportunities.

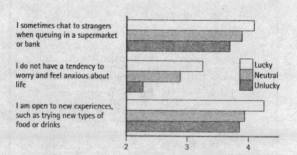

Average scores of unlucky, neutral, and lucky people on the Luck Profile

PRINCIPLE ONE:
Maximize Your Chance Opportunities

Principle: Lucky people create, notice, and act upon the chance opportunities in their lives.

Subprinciples:

1. Lucky people build and maintain a strong "network of luck."

2. Lucky people have a relaxed attitude toward life.

3. Lucky people are open to new experiences in their lives.

Increasing the Luck in Your Life

The following techniques and exercises will help to enhance the degree to which you create, notice, and act upon chance opportunities. Read through them and think about how you can incorporate them into your daily routine. In Chapter Eight I will describe a systematic program explaining how they can be best used to increase the good fortune in your life.

1. Build and maintain a strong "network of luck."

Think back to Robert—the lucky aircraft safety officer who constantly bumps into people who have a very positive effect on his life. The secret of Robert's success is that he enjoys being with people. He likes spending time with friends, going to parties, and chatting with strangers in supermarket lines. And the more people he meets, the greater the likelihood of his encountering a "chance" opportunity. In addition, lucky people like Robert also have a kind of social magnetism—people are attracted to them because of their body language. Think more about your body language in your social life and at work. Make smiling a habit. Smile when you see someone you know or someone that you would like to make contact with. Don't try to fake it by putting on a false smile. Instead, think about how you genuinely feel. Also, force yourself to adopt an "open" posture. Uncross your arms and legs and keep your hands away from your face. Initiate and maintain friendly amounts of eye contact. Open up and have fun trying to attract people to you. Finally, you may remember how lucky people also invest a great deal of effort in keeping in touch with the people that they meet. Remember how Kathy describes herself as a "people collector" and could gather together fifty friends from all parts of her life to celebrate her birthday? I want you to do the same. Make a real effort to connect with more people, use your body language appropriately to attract people to you, and stay in touch with friends and colleagues.

SUGGESTED EXERCISES

Connect Four

Each week for the next month, I would like you to strike up a conversation with at least one person who you don't know very well, or don't know at all. Although lucky people find it relatively easy to talk to people that they do not know, most people find it quite difficult. Here are some tips about the best way to go about it.

- Do not try to talk to people who make you feel uncomfortable; instead, try to initiate a conversation only with people who look friendly and approachable.

- Try to avoid making your opening gambit look artificial and contrived. Instead, capitalize on a naturally occurring situation, such as when you find yourself standing next to someone in a line, or happen to be in the same section of a bookstore, or sit next to someone on a train or airplane.

- To break the ice, ask the person for information or help. In a store you might ask if she knows when the store closes, in the street you might ask for directions or whether he knows a good place to eat. Alternatively, find something about the person that you like, or find interesting, and comment on it. At a party you might notice that someone is wearing a sweater that you really like and ask her where she bought it. In a coffee shop you might see that someone has a book that you have been thinking about reading; ask what he thinks of it. Use open, rather than closed, questions. Closed questions can be answered with a simple yes or no and do not encourage conversation. Open questions require longer, more descriptive answers and often act as a natural springboard for interaction. For example, "Do you like Tolkien?" is a closed question, whereas "What do you think of Tolkien?" is an open question.

- If the person seems friendly, elaborate on your opening gambit. Tell him why you needed to know when the store closes, why you want directions to a certain place, or why you were thinking of reading a particular book. If you get on really well, suggest meeting up again. Don't be afraid of being direct and just asking the person if she would like to meet for coffee sometime, or perhaps think about inviting her to a party or to the movies with your friends.

- Most important of all—don't be afraid of rejection. Your first few attempts may simply involve a brief interaction and nothing more. Don't take it personally—perhaps the person was busy or just didn't feel like chatting—instead, keep on going. There are lots of people out there and many will be delighted that you made the effort to talk to them.

Play the Contact Game

Each week, I would like you to make contact with one person who you haven't been in touch with for a while. Many people find this difficult. Here are some ideas about how to do it.

Look through your address book and make a list of the names and telephone numbers of all the people that you haven't spoken to for a while. Go back over your past school, work, and community connections. Make the list as long as possible. Then, each week play the "ten-minute contact game." Give yourself ten minutes to talk to someone that you haven't spoken to for a while. Choose someone, pick up the telephone, and call that person. If the person answers the call, have a chat with him—explain that you felt bad about not being in contact, ask him how he is and what has been happening in his life. If he doesn't answer the telephone, then quickly find another candidate from your address book and call her. You have ten minutes to talk to someone that you haven't spoken to for a while. And your time starts now.

2. Develop a more relaxed attitude toward life.

Anxious people tend to have a very narrow focus of attention and so often fail to notice the opportunities that surround them. Think back to the newspaper experiment that I described earlier on. Recall how everyone missed an opportunity to win $250 simply because each person was so focused on counting pictures. Lucky people are more relaxed about life and therefore notice the opportunities around them. Also, it is not only a case of how you look, but where you look. You may remember how lucky people often come across life-changing opportunities in newspapers and magazines. Lynne's entire life changed when she came across an article in a local newspaper about a woman who had won a few competition prizes. That article eventually led Lynne to win several large prizes in national competitions and achieve her lifelong ambition of being a successful freelance writer. Other lucky people spoke about the important opportunities that they have come across by surfing the Internet and listening to the radio. I would like you to incorporate these techniques into your life—be more relaxed and receptive to the many opportunities that surround you on a daily basis. Try to look at the world through the eyes of a child, without expectations and prejudice. See what is there rather than what you expect to be there. Relax. Have fun. Go create. Do not let your expectations limit your vision. If you go to a party totally focused on meeting your perfect partner, you might miss a wonderful opportunity to make a lifelong friend. Remember that you are surrounded by opportunities. It is just a case of looking in the right places and seeing what is really there.

SUGGESTED EXERCISE

Relax, Then Do It

Many lucky people described using various forms of relaxation techniques to lower their stress levels. This exercise is one of the best; it will help you adopt a more relaxed approach to life and lower the tension in your body and mind. Carry out the following exercise right now, and then run through it each time you feel yourself becoming anxious.

First of all, find a quiet room or place. Next, close your eyes and take a few deep breaths. Now imagine yourself in a scene that you find relaxing. Perhaps you are lying on a sun-drenched beach. Perhaps you are walking through a leafy glade on a summer day. Perhaps you are looking out on a perfectly still lake. In your mind, create whatever scene makes you feel calm and happy. Imagine what it would look like. Imagine what you would hear if you were really there. The sound of the sea on the shore. The sound of the birds in the trees. The wind in the trees. Imagine the grains of sand against your fingertips. The smell of the clean country air. Imagine yourself taking in all aspects of your surroundings—not just what you want to see and hear, but all aspects of what is there, the sounds, the shapes, the colors, the smells.

Now imagine all of the tension in your body slowly dripping away. Imagine it flowing down through your body and out through your feet and hands. Start with your head. Relax the muscles in your face as you feel the tension and stress fall away. Now gently move your head from side to side, and then up and down. Let your shoulders become relaxed and free. Gently shake your arms and hands as you imagine the tension flowing out through the tips of your fingers. Take another deep breath and let your upper body relax. Gently shake each of your legs and imagine them becoming relaxed and free. Spend a few moments letting a feeling of total calm move through your body.

Finally, slowly open your eyes and gently return to the real world. Think about how you feel now compared to before the exercise. Think of how you feel far more relaxed and open. This is a vitally important way of being. It is a powerful state that will be beneficial for your body, your mind, and your luck.

The more you repeat the exercise, the quicker you will be able to obtain this relaxed, open state. So whenever you feel stressed and anxious, simply find a few quiet moments and run through the exercise. You'll be amazed at what happens.

3. Be open to new experiences in your life.

Many lucky people maximize the likelihood of encountering chance opportunities by being open to new experiences. They regularly try different routes to and from work and sometimes even have fun by making random decisions using dice. Remember the analogy of collecting apples in an orchard, which explains how these sorts of behaviors can quickly increase the chance opportunities that people encounter in their lives. Introduce these sorts of techniques into your life and see what happens. Be open to new experiences, vary your routines, and even consider basing minor decisions on the roll of a die. Visit new parts of the orchard and see how many apples you can find.

SUGGESTED EXERCISE

Play the Dice Game

Make a list of six new experiences— things that you have never done before but wouldn't mind trying. Some of the experiences might be fairly simple, such as trying a new type of food or going to a new restaurant. Others might be more adventurous, such as going bungee jumping or hang gliding. Some could be deliberately lighthearted, such as playing a round of mini golf or visiting the zoo. Some might require more prolonged effort, such as learning a new language, signing up for an evening class, joining a gym, or doing some volunteer work for an organization. You might choose others because they push back your comfort zone—perhaps you might think about taking swimming lessons if you have avoided them in the past because you are afraid of water. Or perhaps the experience will fulfill a long-held secret desire—if you have always wanted to join a circus, then you might consider signing up for a weekend course on clowning.

Write down a list of the experiences and number them 1 to 6. Next, find a die. Now comes the really important moment. You have to make a promise to yourself. You have to promise that you will roll the die and carry out whichever experience is selected. You are not allowed to swap the experience for another one or decide to back out. At this point, you might want to go back and alter your possible experiences. That's fine. But once you have decided upon your final list, you have to roll the die and carry out the chosen option.

Now make the list, roll the die, and enjoy the experience.

CHAPTER FOUR

Principle Two: Listen to Your Lucky Hunches

Principle:
Lucky people make successful decisions by using their intuition and gut feelings.

Marilyn, a twenty-six-year-old sales representative, was typical of many of the unlucky people involved in my research. Her bad luck manifests itself in many different areas of her life. But much of Marilyn's bad luck centers around her love life. Marilyn met her first boyfriend, Scott, while working at a bar in

Spain. He was nineteen years old and had just arrived from Britain for a two-week vacation. On his first night in town, he walked into the bar where Marilyn was working and the two of them started to chat. They got on well and saw a great deal of each other over the coming weeks. At the end of his vacation, Scott told Marilyn that he had fallen in love with her and was willing to come to Spain to be with her. A few weeks later he flew back to Spain with his belongings and moved in with Marilyn.

Marilyn thought that she had met her perfect partner. It seemed like a fairy-tale romance, and at first, everything went very well. But after a few months the relationship started to go wrong. Scott began to treat Marilyn very badly. He became selfish, insulting, and arrogant. Marilyn thought that the problems were due to Scott being so far away from home and suggested that they move back to Britain. A few months later the two of them flew back to London and Marilyn hoped that their relationship would

> "Those who have succeeded at anything and don't mention luck are kidding themselves."
>
> —LARRY KING

improve. Instead, everything went from bad to worse. Scott continued to treat her badly, and the situation quickly deteriorated. Marilyn eventually ended the relationship when she discovered that Scott had been seeing other women.

Shortly afterward, Marilyn met John. The relationship started off well and the two of them moved in together. Again, everything ended in disaster. After a few months of living with each other, John lost his job and Marilyn had to try to support the two of them on her small student grant. When John did eventually find a job, he frequently didn't bother to turn up at work. He started to borrow large amounts of money from Marilyn but rarely paid back the loans. When the relationship finally ended, Marilyn was left thousands of dollars in debt.

Lucky people's choice of partner tends to be far more successful. Like many of the lucky people involved in my work, Sarah has also been very fortunate in her love life. During college, she joined the Officer Training Corps and, at the very first meeting, found herself chatting to the young instructor who was teaching her how to strip and clean a self-loading rifle. Immediately they both knew that they were made for each other. She broke off her existing engagement and married the instructor. It was a brave decision, but Sarah was convinced that she was doing the right thing. The test of time has proved that she made the correct choice— the two of them have now been happily married for more than twenty-seven years.

Interestingly, lucky people's ability to make successful decisions and choices also manifests itself in their professional lives. They consistently place their trust in colleagues and clients who are honest and reliable, and they make sound choices when it comes to their careers and financial matters. Unlucky people are the opposite. They tend to make poor business decisions, trust unreliable people, buy shares just before the stock market crashes, and back horses that fall at the first fence.

When I asked lucky and unlucky people what was behind their successful and unsuccessful decisions, they had very little idea how to explain their consistent good and bad fortune. Lucky people said that they simply knew when a decision was right. In contrast, unlucky people viewed many of their poor decisions as yet more evidence of how they were always destined to fail. I undertook research to discover why lucky people's decisions led to so much more success and happiness than those of unlucky people. The results show the remarkable abilities of our unconscious minds.

Let's start with an unusual demonstration.

John is a multimillionaire because of his ability to predict the stock market accurately and reliably.

For the past ten years, Bill's market predictions have been consistently sound and resulted in very large profits.

This page and the next contain illustrations and short descriptions of six imaginary financial analysts. All of these people have spent many years investing in the stock market. Some of them have been very successful and others have not. I would like you to read each of the descriptions, look at the corresponding illustrations, and spend just a few seconds imagining what each analyst would be like as a person. After you have looked at all six people, please return to this page.

Have you looked at all six? Now I'm going to introduce you to two more financial analysts. Imagine that both of them are going to give you financial advice about how best to invest your savings. You have never met them before and know nothing about their background. I would like you to take a quick look at their faces and decide whose advice you would follow. Don't

Eric's predictions about the stock market have consistently failed and he has developed a reputation as a very poor analyst.

Norman has lost vast sums of money because of his poor ability to predict the stock market.

think about it too long—just quickly look at them, make a decision, and then return to this page. The illustrations of these two new analysts are shown in Appendix B, on page 351.

Jack has an uncanny ability to know which stocks will do well and his investments have made millions of pounds.

David is now considering a change of career because his market predictions have consistently performed so badly.

Remember which analyst you selected. Before we examine the significance of your choice, we need to look at my initial research into the mystery of why lucky people make sound decisions.

Subprinciple 1:
Lucky people listen to their gut feelings and hunches.

I examined many different aspects of the way in which lucky and unlucky people made decisions: how they assessed evidence, thought about different options, and chose one alternative over another. Initially, I could find almost no differences between the two groups. Then I decided to examine whether lucky and unlucky people differed on a rather mysterious aspect of decision making, namely, intuition.

Most feelings are relatively easy to define. We know what someone means when he says that he feels happy, sad, angry, or calm. But it is much harder to know exactly what people are referring to when they talk about intuition. Part of the problem is that different people use the word in different ways. For some, intuition is responsible for that "Eureka" moment that seems to pop out of nowhere. Other people use the same word to describe a form of creativity. Artists, poets, and writers often refer to their intuitive abilities when they talk about the creative processes that lie behind their paintings, poems, and books.

I wasn't interested in these types of intuition. Instead, I wanted to explore the ways in which we use intuition to make important life decisions—the rather curious sensation that something we have just done, or are about to do, is very right or very wrong. Is the person we have just met our perfect partner or an untrustworthy charlatan? Will a risky business decision work out fine or be a complete disaster? I wondered whether lucky people use their intuition more often than unlucky people. If so, did they use it in all areas of their lives or only for certain types of decisions? To uncover answers to some of these questions I decided to conduct a survey. I had over a hundred lucky and unlucky people answer a short questionnaire concerning the role of intuition in their lives.[1] The questionnaire asked everyone to indicate whether they used their intuition when making decisions in four specific areas of their lives, namely, their careers, their personal relationships, business, and finance.

The results were fascinating. As you can see in the following graph, a large percentage of lucky people used their intuition when making decisions in two of the four areas mentioned on the questionnaire. Almost 90 percent of lucky people said that they trusted their intuition when it came to their personal relationships, and almost 80 percent said that it played a vital role in their career choices. Perhaps more important, a greater percentage of lucky than unlucky people reported trusting their intuition in all four areas. And often these differences were far from trivial. About 20 percent more lucky than unlucky people used their intuition when it came to making important financial decisions, and over 20 percent more used their intuition when thinking about their career choices.

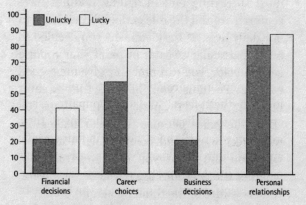

Percentage of unlucky and lucky people using intuition
when making decisions in various areas of their lives

These results suggested an important link between luck and intuition. Far more lucky than unlucky people were relying on their intuition when it came to making important decisions in their lives. It was a simple message—when it came to luck, intuition mattered. But these results also created more questions than answers. Were lucky people's gut feelings especially accurate and reliable? And if so, why was this the case? And why did unlucky people make intuitive decisions far less frequently than lucky people? To find out more, I had to delve deep into the subconscience.

More than a hundred years of psychological research has uncovered a great deal about the way we think, feel, and behave.[2] Some of the most surprising and intriguing findings have centered around the role of the subconscience in our daily lives. If I ask you why you decided to buy a particular sweater or paint your room a certain color, you can probably give me a good reason. Perhaps you bought the sweater because you liked the pattern on it. Perhaps you chose the paint because the color makes the room feel warm and comfortable. You know why you did what you did. Regardless of whether the decisions are trivial or significant, you are aware of the thinking behind them.

Or at least you think you are. But what if all of this was simply an illusion? What if many of the important decisions in your life have been influenced by factors outside of your consciousness? It may sound like a movie plot or a conspiracy theory, but the results of hundreds of psychological experiments suggest that it is true. We are conscious of only a tiny fragment of the factors that influence the way we think, decide, and behave. Instead, we are often driven by our subconscience.

Let's consider a straightforward way in which the subconscience influences some people's decisions. We all have wants and desires. Most people would like to find their perfect partner or discover an easy way of making lots of money. For some people, these desires can exert a powerful influence over how they view the world and can even cause them to see what they want to see rather than what is actually right in front of their noses. Their desire to find the perfect partner might make them overlook obvious signs of deceit or incompatibility. And their need to make easy money might cause them to invest in an obvious scam or confidence game. But subconsciously, these people often realize that they are deceiving themselves into believing what they want to believe. Deep down, they know that something is wrong. And often this rather odd feeling emerges as a kind of intuition—an inner voice or gut feeling telling them that they are kidding themselves. Some people listen to this inner voice and others choose to continue with their wishful thinking and self-denial. Either way, this is a straightforward example of how our subconscience has the power to influence the way we think, feel, and behave. But it is far from the full story. In fact, it is only the tip of the iceberg.

Let's return to the example of you buying your sweater and choosing the paint for your room. It feels like you are well aware of why you bought what you bought. To some extent, this is probably true. You bought the sweater because you liked the pattern. You chose the paint because you liked the color. But why do you like the pattern on that sweater more than the patterns on other sweaters? Why do you prefer red paint to pink paint? To what extent are these preferences guided by your subconscience?

A large amount of research has investigated exactly this issue and produced some rather surprising results. In one well-known study, experimenters showed people lots of squiggles written on pieces of paper. They were just a series of meaningless patterns. A short while later, the experimenters showed everyone a very long list of squiggles. Some of the squiggles were the same ones that people had seen before, others were completely new to them. Everyone was asked to try to identify which ones they had seen before and which ones were new.

The experimenters discovered that squiggles are difficult to remember, and people were unable to identify which were familiar.

Next, the experimenters simply asked everyone to indicate which squiggles they preferred. Some squiggles were appealing to people and others were equally unappealing. But when the experimenters looked at the patterns that had appealed to people, they discovered something surprising. Without realizing it, people consistently said that they preferred the squiggles that they had seen in the first part of the experiment. They didn't consciously remember seeing these squiggles, but for some reason they simply preferred them. And even more interesting was the fact that participants came up with all sorts of reasons to justify their decisions. Some said that they had chosen certain squiggles because they were more aesthetically pleasing than others; others said that the squiggles simply "felt" right. Incredibly, almost no one had any insight into the real factor that had actually influenced their decisions—namely, that the squiggles that they preferred were the ones that they had seen before.[3]

This finding cannot be dismissed as a fluke because psychologists have discovered this phenomenon time and time again, both inside and outside the laboratory. This "familiarity" effect is not limited to squiggles. Without realizing it,

we all prefer things that we have seen before.[4]
The phenomenon affects many aspects of our
everyday thinking and behavior. It is part of the
theory behind branding and explains why com-
panies are willing to spend millions of dollars
on advertising campaigns to keep their products in the public eye. Our subconscience guides
many of our everyday choices—from the
sweaters we buy to the colors that we paint our
rooms, from the products that we choose to the
supermarkets that we use.

Have you ever been introduced to someone
and instantly had a strong feeling about him?
You don't know what it is, but there is just
something about him. That "something" might
be positive. You might really like him. You
might instantly feel that you can trust him.
Alternatively, the feeling might be negative. You
don't know why, but you simply don't trust him.
These sorts of intuitive impressions often dic-
tate how long we speak to someone, whether we
would like to see him again, whether we trust
him, and whether we would want to do business with him. And the results of recent experiments suggest that these types of decisions also
depend on the hidden workings of our subconscious minds. Some of this research has been
conducted very recently. In fact, one study was
carried out on you in the last fifteen minutes.

YOUR LUCK JOURNAL: EXERCISE 7

The Role of Intuition in Your Life

This exercise is designed to assess the degree to which your intuition, lucky hunches, and gut feelings have played an important role in your life.

At the top of a new page in your Luck Journal, write the heading "Times when I was glad that I followed my intuition."

Think back to the times when you can remember that you had a strong intuitive feeling about a person or situation, acted upon that feeling, and are now glad that you did. Perhaps when you were first introduced to your partner, you simply knew that you were right for each other and have now enjoyed a long and happy relationship together. Or maybe you suddenly had a gut feeling that an apparent close friend was not to be trusted, held back from sharing some especially private information with her, and then later found out that she had been spreading gossip about you behind your back. Perhaps your intuition concerned an event in your professional life. Maybe you felt certain that a particular career move was right and, even though everyone else advised you against it, acted on your hunch and landed your dream job.

Write a brief description of each of these events in your Luck Journal.

Now, at the top of the next page in your journal, please write the title "Times when I failed to follow my intuition and lived to regret it."

This time, think about any instances when you experienced a strong gut feeling about a person or situation, didn't take any action, and now wish that you had. Perhaps you had a gut feeling that your partner was cheating on you but carried on in a relationship and later found out that he or she had indeed been unfaithful. Or perhaps you went ahead with a business deal despite having a strange feeling that something was wrong, and now wish that you had listened to your inner voice.

Look at the events that you have written on each page of your Luck Journal. When most people complete this exercise they realize that their intuition has played a vital role in some of the most important decisions in their lives. Many people also realize that some of their biggest failures in life have been due to a reluctance to listen to their inner voice. Imagine what it would be like to live a life in which your intuitive feelings were far more frequent and accurate, a life in which your hunches acted as a reliable alarm bell that something was right or wrong.

Remember the various financial analysts that you saw toward the start of the chapter? Well, this was a simple demonstration designed to discover whether your impressions about people might be influenced by your subconscience. I asked you to look at the illustrations of six imaginary financial analysts. Some were successful and others were unsuccessful. Next, I asked you to look at illustrations of two more analysts and decide whose advice you would accept if you were going to invest your savings. Look again at the two illustrations in Appendix B, on page 351. My prediction is that you will have accepted the advice of Analyst 1 and rejected the advice of Analyst 2. This decision is based on a similar experiment I carried out at my laboratory, when Analyst 1 was selected by 90 percent of participants. The results showed that the test works with most people. It also revealed that most people did not know why they made their choice. It just felt like a hunch.

This demonstration is based upon an ingenious experiment carried out by psychologist Thomas Hill and his colleagues at the University of Tulsa.[5] At the start of this chapter, there was a relationship between the six initial faces of the financial analysts and how successful their investments had been. People with long faces i.e., those whose features were positioned higher in their face, were described as successful and people with shorter faces i.e., those whose features were positioned lower in their face were labeled as unsuccessful. Without your realizing it, your subconscience may have detected these differences and then influenced the way in which you evaluated the two new financial analysts. Analyst 1, who most people tend to prefer, had a long face. The previous long-faced analysts you saw were described as successful, and this may have subconsciously influenced your choice. You may have thought that your choice of one analyst over the other was simply a guess. Or perhaps you had a gut feeling that one of the analysts was more competent than the other. But in reality, these decisions may have been based on the remarkable ability of your subconscious mind to detect patterns.[6]

Of course, these experiments have involved only very simple, and somewhat artificial, patterns of faces and descriptions. In my demonstration, successful financial analysts had long faces and unsuccessful ones had short faces. In the real world this is not the case, and it would be wrong to judge a person simply by their facial appearance. In fact, the experiment conducted by Thomas Hill and his colleagues was designed, in part, to show how this sort of thinking can lead us astray. They argued that after seeing a few people who just happen to fit a pattern, we might generalize the same pattern to the people that we meet in the future.

But exactly the same processes can result in intuitions that are far more accurate. In reality, certain types of people do behave in certain ways. And our subconscious minds have a remarkable ability to detect these patterns and set off an intuitive alarm bell when a situation or person suddenly feels very right or very wrong. My interviews suggested that lucky people's gut feelings and hunches tended to pay off time and time again. In contrast, unlucky people often ignore their intuition and regret their decision.

Earlier I mentioned unlucky Marilyn. She has had two serious relationships, the first with Scott, the second with John. Both had been terrible disasters. I asked Marilyn if she had had any intuitive feelings about the relationships before they had started. She told me that her intuition hadn't just spoken to her, it had screamed at her. When Scott moved to Spain, Marilyn went to the airport to meet him. She described how her inner voice had told her that something felt very wrong:

> I saw him walking around with his baggage cart and my first instinct was, "Just hide, don't let him see you, go back." He didn't see me and I thought "No, don't go over there and meet him, just go out and get back in the car."

Marilyn ignored her gut feeling and regrets it. Interestingly, she also had similar feelings throughout her time with Scott in Spain. Instead of acting on them, she continued to live in hope and wait for Scott to grow up:

> I did love him, but not for who he was, but for what I wanted him to be, and what I thought he would be. I was looking into the future and hoping that he would grow up.

Despite her intuition that something was very wrong, Marilyn remained with Scott for nearly a year and a half. Her second relationship with John also ended in misery. Again, Marilyn feels that her intuition about the relationship was sound, but that she simply didn't listen to it:

> I knew what John was like, and that he was lying his head off to me. He just kept making up these really bizarre stories and I knew they weren't true. I never trusted John from the day I was with him, never, never trusted him ... but I still went ahead with the relationship because I was lonely. London can be a horrible place to live and I suppose I needed him.

It's not all about love. Many unlucky people described how they had regretted not following their intuition in other areas of their lives.

Lucky people were just the opposite. They frequently described trusting their intuition and being successful. In Chapter Two we met Lee, who has escaped serious injury on several occasions and is a very successful marketing manager. Lee can vividly remember the strong gut feeling he experienced the moment he first met his wife. Right away, Lee's intuition told him that they were made for each other. And his gut feeling proved to be uncannily accurate—the two of them have been happily married for twenty-five years.

And he is not the only lucky person involved in my work to describe this type of experience. At the start of this chapter I mentioned how Sarah instantly knew when she had met the man of her dreams at the Officer Training Corps. Linda, a forty-five-year-old teacher, described a very similar experience. When she was in her twenties she was engaged to a man that she had met in Kenya. She came back to Britain to gather up her belongings before sailing back to get married. The trip should have taken only a few weeks, but the unexpected closure of the Suez Canal meant that Linda was trapped on the ship for a month. While on board, she met another passenger and simply knew that this was the man of her dreams. She canceled the wedding in Kenya, married the new love of her life, and the two of them have been happily married for many years.

Lucky people's intuition, gut feelings, and hunches can play a crucial role in their lives. In fact, sometimes they may have made the difference between life and death.

Eleanor is a twenty-four-year-old dancer from California. She is convinced that one of her lucky hunches saved her life. She was driving back to her parents' home one night when she noticed a motorcyclist behind her. From the rather strange way that he was driving she assumed that he was lost. When she stopped at her parents' house, the motorcyclist pulled up alongside her car. She told me what happened next:

> I know this sounds really strange, but when I rolled down the window I immediately knew that it was bad news. It was just something that I felt very strongly. I've only experienced this feeling a few times in my life and I just suddenly knew. I suddenly felt very cold. He didn't lift up his visor. It was very threatening, and there was this coldness I can't explain. I can't explain it, but I knew he had a gun and wanted to kill.

She wasn't quite sure what to do, but knew that she shouldn't get out of the car. She slowly reached for her keys and started the ignition. The motorcyclist appeared to become nervous and drove off. When she got into the house, she called the police and explained what had happened. Two days later, a police officer in the next city stopped the same motorcyclist. The man drew a gun and killed the officer. The police later caught him and found out that Eleanor's mystery motorcyclist was a gang member with little regard for the lives of others. Eleanor is convinced that her intuitive decision to start the car saved her life.

David, a thirty-two-year-old participant from Chicago, has spent much of his life working as a builder. In one interview, he described how his gut feeling had almost certainly saved him from serious injury, and possibly death:

I was working on the roof of this mansion in Chicago. It was a big roof, with towers and turrets. It was winter and had just been snowing, and I was working on different parts of the roof when I saw that the roof had a twenty-foot-square well. The well was all covered in about three inches of snow and was about seven feet below the main level of the roof. It just looked like part of the felted roof, and I was just about to jump into it when I suddenly stopped myself. I don't know why, but I just didn't jump. Instead, I just kept looking around the roof. But it was only when I went back in the building and looked up that I saw that the well was actually a huge skylight—a massive piece of glass in the roof. It had been covered in snow and so I hadn't been able to see the glass—but if I'd jumped then I would have gone through the glass and dropped sixty feet into a spiral staircase. And, the amazing thing is, it's totally against my nature not to have jumped down into that little well. I don't know why, but something stopped me. It just didn't feel right.

Without realizing it, David's subconscious expertise about buildings may have triggered a lucky hunch that saved his life.

Other lucky people described how they use their intuition to help them succeed in the workplace. Lee the salesman attributes much of his business success to his accurate hunches about potential customers and staff. He told me about one time that he was so convinced about his intuition that he even went against the opinions of his colleagues:

> We had a telephone call from a potential customer who wanted some information, and everyone else thought it wasn't worth even discussing. I spoke to the man, and there was something about what he was looking for, I've no idea what it was, that made me think, "I've got to go with this and get what he wants." So I put myself out to get what this man wanted, which was a very small order. Everyone advised me that I was wasting my time, but I just was determined to get the order to the man. In fact, I worked right through the night to get it for him by about one o'clock in the morning, and I delivered it myself. Within twelve months I had $250,000 worth of orders from that

man. And the company was now obviously delighted. I am a good judge of personality and have learned to trust my intuition. I've also trained new recruits in sales and marketing, and the ones that I thought were going to be good have usually become very good in the business.

In the previous chapter we met Robert, who works as an aircraft safety officer. His job involves trying to diagnose what is wrong with an aircraft. Large aircraft are obviously very complex machines, and sometimes finding faults is a difficult and very time-consuming process. But Robert has a knack for intuitively knowing what is wrong with an aircraft:

I work in avionics—instruments, electronics, radio, transducers, transmitters, black boxes, and so on. Sometimes, if it is intricate and very complicated, you scratch your head and think, "What on earth could be the problem?" After many years of working on aircraft, I don't know if it is the fact that I know my way around them, but I often have a feeling that I can just pick out the bits that are malfunctioning. Out of a huge aircraft system, I can pinpoint things that are wrong.

Often his colleagues spend hours going through all of the different things that might be wrong with the aircraft. But Robert simply trusts his intuition about where to look first. Time after time his lucky hunches have been amazingly accurate. Robert's intuitive hunches are based on years of working with complex avionics systems. His subconscious mind has managed to learn more about these systems than he is able to consciously explain.

James works for a large city bank and negotiates large-scale corporate loans. He has a reputation among his colleagues for being lucky, and in one interview, he explained that much of his good fortune is due to his trusting his intuition:

> I often have to make important decisions about whether to make large loans to potential customers, and often rely on my intuition. I usually use it as a kind of alarm bell— a reason to go away and dig deeper. I can remember in one particular case, a company came to me asking for a large loan. They looked good on paper and their negotiators came across well in meetings. But something just felt wrong, and it made me reluctant to sign off on the deal. Everyone advised me to give them the loan, but I decided to delay for a couple of days and have my team

make some more inquiries. We took a very detailed look at lots more documentation and conducted more extensive research into the company. Suddenly a very different picture emerged. The company had severe financial problems, but had managed to hide them from us. I went back and turned down their application for the loan. It was one of the best decisions of my career—a few weeks later the information that we found was announced in the press and the company was involved in a big scandal.

Intuition has also been important in creating luck in my own life. A few years ago I was asked to speak at a business conference being held by a large bank. The timing of the talk meant that I had to stay overnight in the hotel attached to the conference center. When I checked into the hotel, the clerk behind the desk asked to take an imprint of my credit card to pay for the room. I have been in this situation hundreds of times before and usually hand over my card without really thinking about it. But this time I suddenly felt uneasy about the situation. I had no idea why I felt so uncomfortable, but I was simply reluctant about handing over my card. In fact, the intensity of the feeling was such that I took the very unusual step of paying for the room with a check. The following day I gave my talk and returned home. A few weeks later I received a rather mysterious message from the conference organizer asking me if I could check my credit card statement for any irregularities. I checked the statement and it was fine. I called the organizer back, told her that there wasn't a problem, and asked why she had wanted me to check. The organizer explained that an employee at the conference hotel had recently been arrested for his part in a large-scale credit card fraud. In fact, several conference delegates who had stayed at the hotel had fallen victim to the scam and found that very large amounts of money had been incorrectly charged to their cards.

I suspect that my years spent looking into the psychology of lying have resulted in a subconscious ability to detect the way that dishonest people behave, and that the clerk had engaged in these behaviors and made me feel that something was wrong. Either way, my intuition saved me a great deal of time, trouble, and possibly money. Interestingly, the conference had been all about how to detect deception in business!

My interviews with lucky people suggested that they are more skilled at making intuitive decisions than unlucky people. Often these decisions concern the people that they meet in their personal and professional lives. Sometimes, they relate to decisions in the workplace. Lucky people's gut feelings and hunches are often surprisingly reliable and accurate. And, even more amazingly, they have no idea what lies behind their success. To them it just looks like luck. In reality, it is all due to the remarkable inner workings of their subconscious minds. By turning my attention to examining why lucky people seem to be more skilled at using their intuition, I discovered in the final phase of this aspect of my research how anyone could learn to make luckier decisions in life.

Subprinciple 2:
Lucky people take steps to boost their intuition.

At the start of this chapter I outlined my survey into luck and intuition. I asked lucky and unlucky people how often they used their intuition and explored the areas of their lives in which they tended to make intuitive decisions. The results showed that lucky people used their intuition more frequently than unlucky people in several important areas, including business, finance, their personal relationships, and their careers. When I prepared the original questionnaire, I realized that knowing the frequency with which people used intuition was only part of the puzzle. I was also interested in discovering whether lucky people did anything to boost their gut feelings and lucky hunches. Before I wrote the questionnaire, I reviewed the main popular books and academic papers on the topic and drew up a list of the most frequently mentioned techniques for promoting intuition. These included a range of methods, such as clearing one's mind of other thoughts, meditation, finding a quiet place, and being contemplative. During the second part of my survey I presented this list to lucky and unlucky people and asked them to indicate which, if any, of the techniques they used on a regular basis.

Once again, the results were fascinating. The following graph shows that a greater percentage of lucky than unlucky people used all of the

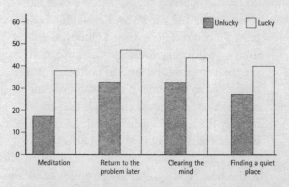

Percentage of unlucky and lucky people using various techniques to boost the role of intuition in their lives

different techniques listed. Some of these differences were very striking; for example, about 20 percent more lucky than unlucky people reported that they engaged in meditation.

My interviews with lucky people illustrated the dramatic impact that these techniques had on their lives.

Nancy is a sixty-four-year-old nurse living in Dallas. She has been lucky in many aspects of her life. She was awarded a scholarship to study nursing and was always lucky when it came to finding jobs that she enjoyed:

> When I came to Dallas I found the perfect job. I was my own boss of a senior wellness program. I could set my own schedule and do my own thing. I stayed there for over ten years. In the last two years, I asked the hospital if I could also develop a clinic for children with learning disabilities, and they gave me the complete freedom to do that. I was probably the only one in that whole organization of several thousand people that could literally do as they wished—with accountability, of course—but it was the perfect job.

In the past, Nancy had not been lucky in all areas of her life. In fact, she had been especially unlucky when it came to love. Now, looking back, she puts much of her ill fortune down to her reluctance to trust her intuition:

> I met my husband straight after I came out of college. I didn't even like him at first. But then he kept pursuing and pursuing and pursuing, and finally I gave in. When I was seeing him, my intuition sent me so many warning bells. I knew it was wrong, even on the day I got married. And then the marriage wasn't good. We were together for thirty-seven years and had five children, but there were many times when I was so discouraged, but I just stuck with it. Eventually, I found the strength to say, "You know, this just isn't working," and finally left. That was a good decision, and I've been really lucky with my children—I have a really good relationship with them.
>
> I had several relationships after the breakup of my marriage. Once again, my intuition rang warning bells but again I ignored them and none of the relationships worked out. But now things are very different. I have really started looking into intuition. I started teaching mental health nursing and I've read a lot about psychology. Now I have more knowledge, more awareness, and more wisdom. And my judgments

and decisions are better. Finally, I have learned my lesson and not gotten into something that would not be right. I listen to my intuition. I think I know exactly how it's going to turn out, and yet I will proceed and examine it and maybe get into it a little bit.

Nancy does not blindly act upon her intuition but instead treats it as a warning to proceed with caution:

Intuition has helped my luck in many different ways. I can just sit by someone at a meeting, or gathering, and I know whether I can trust them. I was looking for a car and I knew exactly which salesman I could trust, and which ones I couldn't trust. I also can spot people who are very needy and I back off from them because they drain my energy.

But it's not just about the people I meet. Twice I've pulled up to a stop sign where normally I would have proceeded. I pulled up even though it was clear. My intuition made me stop—I just suddenly thought, "You know, somebody could go right through this intersection." And both times a car has gone right through in front of me. Both times I would have been in the middle of the intersection and would have been hit. Both times, I think that my intuition may have actually saved my life.

Nancy described how she uses several techniques to boost her gut feelings and lucky hunches:

If the alarm bells have rung, I stand back a little bit and I really look at the situation. I also do some meditation. Usually it's a little difficult to quiet down my mind, but I just say, "What the heck, I'll do it anyway." But I do try to get quiet within. And often I take clues from my dreams. A while back, I took this job with the hospice, and, career-wise, it's a step backward. A few days ago, I had a dream in which I met this woman and she was a political advisor, and I thought what an interesting life she has had. And that I should write about her life because other people would be interested in it. And then I woke up but the dream remained with me. Last year I took a writing class. And I have decided that my intuition is trying to tell me that I am on the wrong path. I thought, "You know, why am I doing this if my spirit isn't in it?" So I'm seriously thinking about quitting the hospice and spending more time writing.

Nancy was not the only lucky person to describe using various techniques to boost her intuition. Jonathan is a forty-year-old director of an international exhibition company. He has had many lucky career breaks and has been happily married to his wife for twenty years. He also has a reputation for having sound intuition when it comes to business decisions:

> About two and a half years ago I had an idea that would work for this international exhibition company. It was for a brand-new concept for pension and investment management. I just saw a gap in the market, made a proposal, and had a strong feeling that there was a demand for it in the exhibition business. I've had many different ideas, but I knew this one just felt right. After some initial reluctance, my company eventually launched it and the feedback from the marketplace has been superb.

During the interview, Jonathan also described the ways meditation has helped promote his intuition:

> I started transcendental meditation a few years ago and I've been doing that regularly every day twice a day . . . twenty minutes twice a day . . . you say a mantra. A friend of

mine started it, and what appealed to me was the fact that it had no dogma, no religion, it's purely a way of getting in touch with your inner self. It's meant to give you all sorts of benefits of energy, concentration, physiology, etc. But I think the one thing it has done for me is increase my levels of intuition and luck. It helps me use my gut feel on all sorts of matters, how to deal with a certain client, make decisions at work, and so on. It helps me to just follow my hunches. And it's not just about decisions at work—it helps in other areas of my life, too—we almost bought a house recently and my gut feeling led me to pull out just at the right moment.

Milton, a thirty-four-year-old teacher from San Diego, also described the important role that intuition played in his life and how he boosted his intuition via meditation:

The only thing wrong with intuition is if you don't listen to it. It's like a butterfly that crosses one's mind, and if you kind of only half listen to it then bad things happen, and you think, "Oh, damn, why didn't I pay attention?" You have to catch it like a butterfly. I've always been into meditation. It definitely helps because it allows your imagination to actually go off and do something which you wouldn't normally be able to do in life. And it encourages you to be relaxed and free. It expands your feelings about other people and helps you be more intuitive and lucky.

YOUR LUCK JOURNAL: EXERCISE 8

Your Luck Profile: Principle Two

It is time to return to the Luck Profile from page xix. Items 4 and 5 on that questionnaire relate to the subprinciples discussed in this chapter. Item 4 asks about the degree to which you listen to your gut feelings and hunches, and Item 5 concerns whether you take steps to attempt to increase your intuitive abilities.

Scoring:

Look back at the ratings you assigned to these two items and then add up these numbers to create a single score (see the following example). This is your score for the second principle of luck.

Statement	Your rating (1–5)
4 I often listen to my gut feelings and hunches.	2
5 I have tried some techniques to boost my intuition, such as meditation or just going to a quiet place.	1
Total for the second principle of luck	3

Now look at the following scale to discover whether your score would be categorized as high, medium, or low. Please make a note of your score and category in your Luck Journal, as these results will become important when we come to discuss how best to enhance the luck in your life.

Low				Medium				High		
2	3	4	•	5	6	7	•	8	9	10

⬡

I have asked a large number of lucky, unlucky, and neutral people to complete the Luck Profile. Lucky people tend to score much higher on these items than other people. Unlucky people tend to obtain the lowest scores (see the following graph).

Average scores of unlucky, neutral, and lucky people on the Luck Profile

Summary

Unlucky people tend to make unsuccessful decisions—they trust the wrong people and make poor career choices. In contrast, lucky people have an uncanny ability to place their trust in reliable and honest people, and make profitable and effective business decisions. These differences depend upon the different ways in which lucky and unlucky people use their intuition when making important decisions in their lives. Unlucky people do not tend to rely upon their gut feelings, hunches, and intuition. It is not that they do not have such feelings, but rather that they do not foster their intuition, nor do they listen to it when it speaks to them. Lucky people are the opposite. They listen to their intuition and use it as an alarm bell—a good reason to stop and consider the situation carefully. Many lucky people also take steps to actively boost their intuitive abilities by meditating and clearing their minds of other thoughts. They have the confidence to trust their inner voices and develop their intuitive feelings. In doing so, they reap the benefits of a lucky life full of successful decisions.

PRINCIPLE TWO:
Listen to Your Lucky Hunches

Principle: Lucky people make successful decisions by using their intuition and gut feelings.

Subprinciples:

1.   Lucky people listen to their "inner voice."

2.   Lucky people take steps to boost their intuition.

Increasing the Luck in Your Life

The following techniques and exercises will help to increase the number of successful decisions you make by using your intuition and gut feelings. Read through them and think about how you can incorporate them into your daily routine. In Chapter Eight I will describe a systematic program explaining how they can be best used to increase the good fortune in your life.

1. Listen to your "inner voice."

Think back to the survey that I conducted into luck and intuition. It revealed that lucky people trust their intuition when it comes to their careers, work, finances, and relationships. And time and time again, these decisions pay off. Remember how marketing manager Lee obtained a huge order for his company by following a gut feeling about a client? And recall how Eleanor's intuition about the motorcyclist who pulled up alongside her car may have saved her life? Unlucky people are the opposite—they often describe how they do not follow their gut feelings and then regret their decision. People like Marilyn have endured several terrible relationships despite their inner voices screaming at them to leave. Listen to your inner voice and carefully consider what it is trying to tell you. Treat it as an alarm bell—a reason to stop and carefully consider a situation or decision.

SUGGESTED EXERCISES

Visit the Old Man in the Cave

There are times when you will be faced with a decision and want to hear what your inner voice has to say about each of the possible options. Whenever that happens, try the following exercise.

Find a quiet room and comfortable chair. Sit down, close your eyes, and take a few deep breaths. Imagine yourself being magically transported to the entrance of a cave on a remote mountain. You walk inside the cave and suddenly feel relaxed and content. You feel secure and totally isolated from the outside world. Calm and peaceful. Imagine that there is an old man sitting in the corner of the cave. He invites you to sit opposite him and describe each of your options. But he doesn't want to hear about them in terms of facts and figures. Profit and loss. Logic and reason. Neither does he want to hear about what others think you should do, or what you think you should do out of a sense of duty. Instead, he would like you to simply describe how you feel about each of the options. What feels right and what feels wrong. The conversation will be completely confidential and so you can be totally honest. Don't think about what you would say. Just say it. Right now. Out loud. Tell the old man how you really feel. Now slowly open your eyes.

What did you say about your options? Which of them felt right and which felt wrong? How does this compare with the objective evidence about each of these options?

If the evidence and your feelings are in line, then you have found your answer. If you discovered that you feel uneasy about an option, even though the evidence suggests that it is correct, then it is perhaps best to reconsider the situation. Take some time out and think carefully before moving forward. Perhaps you will decide to ignore the evidence and follow your intuition. Perhaps you will decide to ignore your intuition and follow the evidence. Whatever you decide to do, at least you will have heard your inner voice.

Make the Decision, Then Stop

To find out how you really feel about your options, simply choose one of them and commit your decision to paper. If you are uncertain about whether to finish a relationship, just write a letter to your partner explaining that it is all over. If you are uncertain about whether to hand in your notice at work, just go for it and write your resignation letter. Now stop. How do you feel right now? You are holding your future in your hands. Do you really want to send that letter or is there something inside telling you that it doesn't feel right? Is that your intuition or are you simply afraid of change? When it came to the crunch, what did your inner voice say to you?

2. Take steps to boost your intuition.

My survey into luck and intuition also revealed how lucky people do many different things to enhance their intuition. Some simply clear their minds, while others invest time in more formal forms of meditation. Some go to a quiet place or stop thinking about a problem and return to it at a later date. Many of these ideas are very simple and do not require much effort to incorporate into your life. Consider trying those that appeal to you and see what happens.

SUGGESTED EXERCISE

Make Meditation Matter

Many lucky people such as Jonathan feel that meditation is the simplest way of increasing their intuition. The idea is not to try to develop any intuitive feelings during the meditation itself. Instead, the meditation is a time for clearing your mind of all other thoughts and distractions. It is after the meditation, when your mind is quiet and clear, that your intuition will feel at its best.

Find a quiet room and sit in a comfortable chair. Close your eyes and carry out the relaxation exercise described on page 106. Once you feel calm, silently repeat the same word or phrase over and over and over again in your mind. It doesn't matter what the word or phrase is. It might be the name of a friend, lines from a song, or even the title of this book. The important point is that you constantly repeat the word and thereby clear your mind of all other thoughts. Focus your mind on the word and try to prevent it from wandering on to other topics. At first, this will be far from easy. But stay with it and remember that practice makes perfect. Over time you will find it easier and easier to focus your thoughts and create a sense of stillness. After about ten minutes or so of focused thought, slowly open your eyes.

Try this simple exercise three times a week, for about twenty minutes each time, and see what effect it has on your luck.

CHAPTER FIVE

Principle Three: Expect Good Fortune

**Principle:
Lucky people's expectations
about the future help them fulfill
their dreams and ambitions.**

We all have dreams and ambitions. Some people want to be amazingly successful in business, win the lottery, or travel the world. Others harbor a secret desire to become famous writers, artists, or movie stars. Most people want to be in loving relationships, many would like to find jobs that they enjoy, and everyone wants to be healthy. My research revealed that lucky people's dreams and ambitions often become a reality, while unlucky people rarely obtain what they want from life.

Clare's bad luck started when she was very young:

> My father was very busy and my mother kept on having to go to the hospital. My grandmother looked after us, and I had to do the housework before school. When all the other children were out playing I had to work all the time and not go out to play, so I never had any friends or any children to play with. I thought I was losing out on my childhood and I thought that my grandmother was being very strict. I suppose I felt that wasn't fair.

Clare has been unlucky in many aspects of her life, including her career and love life. She has longed to find a job that makes her happy and has tried working in advertising and magazine sales. But she has never been especially successful in any of her jobs or found one that she has really enjoyed. Clare has also always wanted to be in a loving, and long-lasting, relationship. She married her first husband, Ken, when she was twenty, and had two children. A few years later, the relationship started to turn sour when Ken began to physically abuse her and sleep with other women. In 1988, Ken unexpectedly died in a car accident. For many years Clare found it difficult to meet new people, but eventually she met Dick. Unfortunately Dick was unemployed, and so Clare had to work hard to support both him and her children. Three years ago, Dick walked out on her for another woman. After another period of loneliness, Clare met Donald. The relationship started off well, but Donald soon became obsessive and difficult. Clare and Donald remain friends, but they are no longer in a relationship together. Instead, Clare is again both alone and unhappy.

In contrast, Erik, fifty-one, is a very lucky man. Like Clare, Erik has tried many different jobs. He has worked as an office clerk, a coal miner, a taxi driver, and a croupier. Unlike Clare, he has enjoyed them all:

> I've loved everything I've done. One of the things I love in life is driving, and when I was a taxi driver I was being paid to drive somebody else's nice car. Another thing I like to do is play cards. I also worked in a casino as a croupier, so I could gamble with somebody else's money, no risk whatsoever. It was per-

fect—I can't think of a job that I've done
that I haven't enjoyed.

Like Clare, Erik has also always wanted to be
in a wonderful relationship and have a happy
family life. Unlike Clare, his dreams have all
come true. Erik met his wife forty years ago and
immediately knew that they were meant for
each other. They have been happily married ever
since and have three children and seven grand-
children. Erik is very happy with his family life:

> Our grandchildren are an absolute
> delight to us. Our life is so full, I always
> say to people, "I'm the luckiest man you
> will ever meet." There definitely seems to
> be a guardian angel, for want of a better
> word, looking after me.

Clare and Erik are typical of many of the people involved in my research. Although they have
the same sorts of wants and desires, unlucky
people's dreams tend to remain nothing more
than an elusive fantasy, while lucky people are
often able to easily obtain what they want from
life.

My research revealed that lucky people do not
achieve their dreams and ambitions purely by
chance. Nor does fate conspire to prevent

unlucky people from obtaining what they want. Instead, lucky and unlucky people achieve, or fail to achieve, their ambitions because of a fundamental difference in how they think about both themselves and their lives.

Subprinciple 1:
Lucky people expect their good luck to continue in the future.

We all have expectations about the future. Some of us expect to be happy and healthy, others are convinced that they will be miserable and sad. Some people expect to find their perfect partner, others anticipate moving from one failed relationship to the next. Some people think that they will do well in their jobs, others expect to remain at the bottom of the career ladder.

Let me ask you a few questions about your future. On a scale of 0 to 100 percent, where 0 percent indicates that the event will never happen and 100 percent indicates that it is an absolute certainty, what are your chances of achieving one of your lifetime ambitions? Twenty percent? Fifty percent? Seventy percent? And what about the likelihood of having a great time on your next vacation? I was eager to discover how the expectations of lucky and unlucky people compared to one another and to those of people who did not consider themselves especially lucky or unlucky. And when I put these questions to lucky and unlucky people, I received some astounding answers.

I presented all the people in the study with questions about their chances of experiencing various positive life events in the future. Some of the questions concerned events that were fairly general, such as achieving one of their lifetime ambitions. Others were far more specific and asked about the chances of their having a great time on their next vacation or receiving an unexpected visit from a long-lost friend. Some of the questions concerned events that were largely under their control, such as maintaining a good relationship with their family, while others related to events that were largely outside of their control, such as being given $250 to spend on themselves.

YOUR LUCK JOURNAL: EXERCISE 9

Positive Expectations

This is the questionnaire used to assess the positive expectations of participants involved in the Luck Project. Please take a few moments to complete it and see how your scores compare to those of lucky people, unlucky people, and neutral people (that is, people who do not consider themselves especially lucky or unlucky).

At the top of a new page in your Luck Journal, please write the heading "Positive Expectations." Now draw a vertical line down the center of the page. On the left-hand side of the page write the letters A to H in a column. Next, read each of the statements in the questionnaire and write a number between 0 and 100 in the right-hand column to indicate the chances that you will experience the event at some point in the future, where 0 means that you think the event will never happen and 100 means that you think the event will *definitely* happen.

You can use any number from 0 to 100, just remember that a *bigger* number means that you think the event is *more likely* to happen and a *smaller* number means that you think the event is *less likely* to happen.

Please do not spend too much time thinking about any one item and answer as honestly as possible.

Statement	Chances of this happening to you (0–100)
A Having someone tell you that you are talented	
B Looking young for your age when you are older	
C Having a great time on your next vacation	
D Being given $250 just to spend on yourself	
E Achieving at least one of your life's ambitions	
F Developing or maintaining a good relationship with your family	
G Having an out-of-town friend visit you	
H Being admired for your accomplishments	

Scoring:

To score the questionnaire, simply add up the numbers that you have written on the right-hand side of the page and divide the total by 8 (see the following example).

Statement	Chances of this happening to you (0–100)
A Having someone tell you that you are talented	85
B Looking young for your age when you are older	12
C Having a great time on your next vacation	55
D Being given $250 just to spend on yourself	48
E Achieving at least one of your life's ambitions	80
F Developing or maintaining a good relationship with your family	80

G	Having an out-of-town friend visit you	95
H	Being admired for your accomplishments	75
	Total	530
	Score (total divided by 8)	66.25

I have administered this questionnaire to a large number of people.

Low scores are between 0 and 45.

Medium scores are between 46 and 74.

High scores are between 75 and 100.

How do you rate your expectations for positive events in your future?

As shown in the following graph, lucky people's expectations of good things happening to them were far higher than the expectations held by unlucky people.[1] On average, lucky people thought that there was about a 90 percent chance of having a great time on their next vacation, an 84 percent chance of achieving at least one of their lifetime ambitions, and about a 70 percent chance of being given $250 to spend on themselves. All of these expectations were much higher than those expressed by unlucky people.

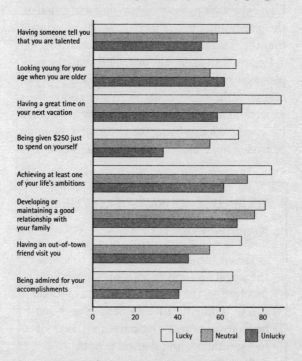

Estimated likelihood of experiencing various positive life events given by unlucky, neutral, and lucky people

And lucky people's high expectations were not just confined to certain questions. Instead, they were certain that they were very likely to experience both general and specific positive events, that were both within and outside of their control. In fact, the lucky people had amazingly high expectations for every single event listed on the questionnaire. In short, they were convinced that the future was going to be fantastic.

I wanted to examine lucky and unlucky people's expectations for negative, as well as positive, events. I therefore asked everyone about their expectations of experiencing a variety of negative life events, such as being the victim of a mugging or having insomnia every night of the week.

YOUR LUCK JOURNAL: EXERCISE 10

Negative Expectations

This is the questionnaire used to assess the negative expectations of participants involved in the Luck Project. Please take a few moments to complete it and see how your scores compare to those of lucky, unlucky, and neutral people.

At the top of a new page in your Luck Journal, please write the heading

"Negative Expectations." Once again, draw a vertical line down the center of the page and on the left-hand side of the page write the letters A to H in a column. Now, read each of the statements in the questionnaire and write a number between 0 and 100 in the right-hand column to indicate the chances that you will experience the event at some point in the future, where 0 means that you think the event will *never* happen and 100 means that you think the event will *definitely* happen.

You can use any number from 0 to 100, just remember that a *bigger* number means that you think the event is *more likely* to happen and a *smaller* number means that you think the event is *less likely* to happen.

Please do not spend too much time thinking about any one item and answer as honestly as possible.

Statement	Chances of this happening to you (0–100)
A Becoming seriously overweight later in life	

B Having insomnia every
   night of the week

C Deciding you chose the
   wrong career

D Having an alcohol problem

E Suffering severe depression

F Attempting suicide

G Being the victim of a
   mugging

H Contracting meningitis

Scoring:

To score the questionnaire, simply add
up the numbers that you have written on
the right-hand side of the page and divide
the total by 8 (see the following example).

Statement	Chances of this happening to you (0–100)
A Becoming seriously overweight later in life	15

B	Having insomnia every night of the week	25
C	Deciding you chose the wrong career	40
D	Having an alcohol problem	2
E	Suffering severe depression	3
F	Attempting suicide	5
G	Being the victim of a mugging	30
H	Contracting meningitis	5
Total		**125**

	Score
(total divided by 8)	15.62

I have administered this questionnaire to a large number of people.

Low scores are between 1 and 10.
Medium scores are between 11 and 25.
High scores are between 26 and 100.

How do you rate your expectations for negative events in your future?

Participants in the study were again asked to rate the likelihood of experiencing each event from 0 percent to 100 percent, and again huge differences emerged between the groups. This time it was the unlucky people who were convinced that they were very likely to experience these events. In

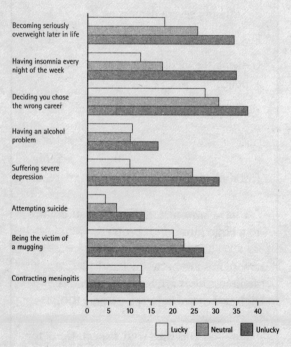

Estimated likelihood of experiencing various negative life events given by unlucky, neutral, and lucky people

fact, unlucky people had higher expectations than lucky people of experiencing every single event on the questionnaire.[2] From suicide to insomnia, and choosing the wrong career to becoming over-weight, unlucky people were far more convinced that it would happen to them.

These simple sets of questions revealed that lucky and unlucky people look at the world in quite different ways. According to lucky people, the future will be bright and rosy. According to unlucky people, it will be bleak and black.

At the start of this chapter I mentioned unlucky Clare and lucky Erik. Like many of the people involved in my research, Clare and Erik shared the same dreams and ambitions. Both had always wanted to be in a loving relationship and find jobs that they enjoyed. But Clare's dreams had remained nothing more than an elusive fantasy while Erik had achieved many of his lifelong ambitions with almost magical ease.

Clare and Erik completed the questions about their expectations for the future. Clare was con-vinced that she was very likely to experience all of the negative life events while Erik was equally certain that he would experience the positive ones. The differences between them were aston-ishing. Clare said that she had a 60 percent chance of becoming seriously overweight in later life, whereas Erik thought that there was simply no chance of this happening to him. Erik said that the likelihood of having a good time on his next vacation was an absolute certainty, while Clare put her chances at just 10 percent. And these very different levels of expectations also emerged in my interviews with the two of them. Like many of the unlucky people, Clare was convinced that she was born unlucky and that her future held nothing but doom and gloom:

> I went to a clairvoyant medium once, and she told me that I was born on the wrong side of Libra. She told me that Libra is the only star sign that's got a negative and a positive side, and told me that I was born on the negative side. I think that anything I want to do will go wrong. Every time I want to do the lottery, I think, "Well, I'm not going to win anyway." In the mid-1980s I wrote two books and now I am in the middle of writing another book. But I started writing it about a year and a half ago and haven't picked it up for about a year—I hope that it will get published, but my expectations aren't too high on getting a publisher.

In contrast, Erik was far more upbeat about what the future had in store for him:

I always go into things believing they'll
work out well. I am convinced that everything will be great. I've certainly come
unstuck, but even then, good things come
out of the bad and I always come out smiling. Some people don't realize their luck
when it is there. They look out of the window and say, "Oh, dear, it's raining today,"
but I see the rain and think, "Great, my
flowers will be out tomorrow."

Lucky and unlucky people have amazingly different expectations about the future. And these
expectations play an absolutely vital role in
explaining why some people obtain their dreams
with uncanny ease, while others rarely get what
they want from life. Before I explain how these
expectations have such a dramatic impact on
people's lives, it is important to understand why
lucky and unlucky people have such different
ideas about what the future has in store for them.

Imagine that a few weeks ago you applied for
your dream job and recently received a letter
inviting you to an interview. After opening the
letter you spend a few minutes reflecting on the
likelihood of being offered the job. You might
think about whether you will be able to anticipate the questions that you are likely to be
asked, whether you have the right skills for the

job, and whether you will be able to perform well in the interview. You probably won't find it especially difficult to answer these questions. You will know whether you are good at preparing for interviews, have the necessary skills for the job, and are good at presenting yourself.

Many of the other factors that will affect your chances of being offered the job are far harder to predict. Perhaps you will arrive late for the interview because of an unforeseen and unavoidable delay. Perhaps you will perform badly after arriving soaking wet due to a sudden and unexpected rain shower. Perhaps you will make a bad first impression by walking into the interview room and accidentally tripping over an upturned edge of a rug. You cannot predict these types of events. They may happen or they may not.

Now imagine what the world would be like if you were exceptionally lucky or unlucky. If you were lucky, all of these apparently unpredictable events would work out in your favor. You would arrive on time, the sun would shine, and the edges of rugs would lie flat on the floor. And if you were unlucky, everything would work out against you. You would be delayed, the storm clouds would gather, and the edge of every rug would rise up against you. In fact, the negative outcome of these seemingly unpredictable events would be one of life's few certainties.

This is one of the reasons why lucky and unlucky people have such wildly different expectations about the future. Lucky people are convinced that these sorts of unpredictable and uncontrollable events will consistently work out for them. Unlucky people are the opposite: They believe events within and outside their control will always work out against them. And, as we saw in Chapter Two, luck affects all aspects of people's lives. It is not just a case of being lucky or unlucky when going for job interviews. Luck also affects people's health, their careers, and their financial well-being. Lucky people are convinced that the sun will always shine on them, whereas unlucky people expect storm clouds to gather in their personal and professional lives.

> "I think that most of the people involved in any art always secretly wonder whether they are really there because they're good or because they're lucky."
>
> —KATHARINE HEPBURN

There is also a second reason why lucky and unlucky people have such extremely different expectations about the future. Most people tend to base their expectations about the future on what has happened in the past. If you have been healthy in the past then you probably expect to be healthy in the future. If you have performed well at job interviews in the past then you will probably expect to perform well in the future. Lucky and unlucky people are exactly the same. Lucky people think that if their flight arrived on time in the past, then it will arrive on time in the future. Unlucky people think that if they have failed job interviews in the past, then they will continue to fail them in the future. But what happens when unlucky people encounter lucky events and lucky people encounter unlucky events? Surely this must make their expectations about the future a little less extreme?

In fact, this is not the case. Instead, something very strange happens. Lucky people see any bad luck in their lives as being very short-lived. They simply shrug it off and don't let it affect their expectations about the future. Unlucky people are convinced that any good luck in their lives will only last for a short period of time and will quickly be followed by their regular dose of bad luck.

Previously we met unlucky Clare. She has been unlucky in love and has never been able to find a job that she enjoyed. I asked her how her expectations about the future would be affected by something lucky happening in her life:

I do think that if something good happens, something bad has got to follow. If something good happened in my life, I would be really shocked because I've had so much bad luck happen. I think if I won a lot of money on the lottery, then I would expect somebody to take it away from me, or I would find out that I hadn't really won, or something. It's a feeling that you get when you've been unlucky all the time. You just can't possibly be lucky.

This viewpoint occurred throughout my interviews with unlucky people. As another unlucky person said:

It almost seems that if things are going right for me, somebody will come along with a big foot and stomp on me and say, "Oh, no, she's having too much fun," and alter the situation. If I'm starting to enjoy myself I've got to be pushed back down again. I always wonder what's going to happen, what's around the corner. I suppose you shouldn't think like that. You should think, "Oh, this is nice, I hope it will last," but I just can't think about it like that.

Unlucky people are convinced that any good

luck that does happen to them will soon fade away, and that their future will continue to be bleak and miserable. Lucky people dismiss any unlucky events in their lives as short-lived and transitory. In doing so, they are able to maintain their expectations of a bright and happy future.

What impact do these unusual and extreme expectations have on people's lives? Our expectations have a powerful effect on the way in which we think, feel, and act. They can influence our health, how we behave toward others, and how others behave toward us. My research revealed that the special kind of expectations held by lucky and unlucky people had a huge impact on their lives. The unique way that the lucky people in my study thought about their future was responsible for their being more effective than most when it came to achieving their dreams and ambitions. Likewise, the negative expectations held by the unlucky people resulted in their being especially ineffectual at getting what they wanted from life. It all came down to the way in which their extreme expectations about the future had the power to become self-fulfilling prophecies.

Imagine that you are feeling a bit down because you have just moved to a new neighborhood and are finding it difficult to meet people. Just for fun, you decide to go to the local fortuneteller to find out what the future holds for you. The fortune-teller takes your money, gazes into her crystal ball, smiles, and says that the future looks bright. She says that within a few months you will be surrounded by many close and loyal friends. You are reassured by the fortuneteller's comments and walk away feeling much happier than when you arrived. Because you now feel happy and confident about the future, you smile more, go out more, and talk to more people. In short, you start to behave in a way that greatly increases your chances of making friends. After a few weeks you find that you are indeed surrounded by a close circle of friends and frequently recommend the fortuneteller to others. In fact, it is quite possible that the fortuneteller did not actually see into the future but instead actually helped to create it. Her comments affected your expectations about your social life and this, in turn, caused you to behave in a way that increased the chances of these expectations becoming a reality. Your expectations became a self-fulfilling prophecy.

Research has shown that these types of self-fulfilling prophecies have the power to affect many areas of our lives. In one famous experiment, psychologists told American high school teachers that certain children in their class had been identified as "late bloomers," and that

these children would probably do especially
well in the future. In fact, there was nothing
special about the children—they had been randomly selected. The researchers then examined
the effect that the teachers' expectations had on
their pupils over the course of a few months.
Without realizing it, the teachers provided
these pupils with more encouragement and
praise and allowed them to ask additional questions in class. This resulted in the randomly
selected "late bloomers" producing much better
schoolwork and obtaining higher scores on
intelligence tests than the other children. The
teachers' expectations had caused them to
behave in a way that transformed their expectations into a reality.[3]

Self-fulfilling prophecies do not just affect
children's levels of success at school. They affect
our health, how we behave in the workplace,
how we behave with others, and how others
respond to us.[4] In fact, they affect many aspects
of our lives much of the time. And my work
revealed that the extremely different expectations held by lucky and unlucky people had the
potential to transform into especially powerful
self-fulfilling prophecies, and this, in turn,
explained why lucky people frequently achieved
their dreams while unlucky people did not.

SUGGESTED EXERCISE

The Power of Expectation

Our expectations affect many aspects of our thoughts and behavior. Have a quick look at the sentence below:

PARIS

IN THE

THE SPRINGTIME

Most people read this sentence as "Paris in the springtime." In fact, if you look carefully, you will see that it actually says "Paris in the the springtime." However, we do not expect to see two *the's* following each other in a sentence, and so we tend to read what we expect to see rather than what is is actually there.

Another ingenious experiment demonstrated that people's expectations can even affect their reaction time. Participants were randomly assigned to one of two groups. People in one group were asked to press a switch the moment that a light came on. They were asked to try as hard as they

could. The other group was told to imagine
that they were fighter pilots with very fast
reactions. They were then given exactly the
same task as the first group, that is, to press
a button whenever a light was illuminated.
Amazingly, the people in the second group
responded much faster than those in the
first group. They expected to do well and
their expectations affected their behavior.
In just the same way, lucky people expect to
do well in life and that expectation plays a
major role in their success.

Subprinciple 2:
Lucky people attempt to achieve
their goals, even if their chances of
success seem slim, and persevere in
the face of failure.

Let's discuss one of the most straightforward
ways in which self-fulfilling prophecies affect
the lives of lucky and unlucky people. In the
previous section I described how unlucky people are often convinced that their lives are going

to be full of failure and misery. They are certain that they will not pass exams or find a job that they enjoy. Worse still, they believe that there is nothing that they can do to affect the bad things that are going to happen to them. They are convinced that they are unlucky and that unlucky people will always experience bad luck. These beliefs can quickly cause them to lose hope and simply give up.

The concept can be illustrated with a simple example. Earlier on in the book we met lucky competition winners Lynne, Joe, and Wendy. All of them won a huge number of prizes, and all put much of their good luck down to the fact that they enter a large number of competitions. As Joe said, "You've got to be in to win." Many of the unlucky people explained that they never entered competitions and lotteries because they were convinced that their bad luck would prevent them from winning. As Lucy, a twenty-three-year-old unlucky student told me:

> I can remember, even when I was little, not entering things because I just never won anything. When I was seven, I was in elementary school at an assembly and my parents were in the audience. My mom had entered a competition for me and they called out the winner and it was me.

But I hadn't entered it, it was my mom.
The way I see it, I hadn't won, she had.

Clearly, unlucky people's expectations about
competitions are very likely to become self-fulfilling prophecies. By not entering competitions, they severely reduce their chances of winning. And exactly the same attitude affects
many important areas of their life. The resulting lack of any attempt to change their lives can
easily turn unlucky people's low expectations
about the future into a miserable reality.

Another unlucky student had a track record
of failing exams and described her expectations
about some exams that she would have to take
in a few months' time:

> I am convinced that I am going to fail my
> exams. I am often just a mess, thinking,
> "There's no point me doing this, I'm going
> to fail." I've not turned up to take exams in
> the past because I just thought there's no
> point, and I've even not bothered preparing
> for exams in the past as well because I have
> been so convinced that I'm going to fail.

Another unlucky man described how he
could never find a job. I asked him to describe
his expectations about the future:

I know that I will never find a job and so never really try to get one anymore. I have given up looking. I used to look through the newspapers every week to see what was available, but now I think, what's the point—I am never going to find anything suitable and even if I do, something will go wrong and that will be that. It's just my bad luck. That's just me.

These comments provide a striking insight into how unlucky people create much of the bad luck in their lives. If they don't attend an exam then they are certain to fail. And if they don't try to look for a job then they will remain unemployed. And if they are reluctant to go on dates then they reduce their chances of finding a partner. They also illustrate the power of self-fulfilling prophecies. Unlucky people are so convinced that they are going to fail that they often do not make any attempt to achieve their goals, and this, in turn, transforms their expectations into a reality.

At one point in my research I conducted a simple experiment to examine how lucky and unlucky people's expectations affected the degree to which they would attempt to achieve a simple goal. I showed both lucky and unlucky people the same two puzzles. Each puzzle consisted of two pieces of metal that were interlocked. I explained that it was possible to unlock the pieces in one puzzle and impossible to unlock the pieces in the other puzzle, but didn't tell them which puzzle was which. I then explained that I had tossed a coin beforehand to determine which puzzle they would be asked to solve, and then handed them one of the puzzles. In fact, everyone was given the same puzzle. I asked them to simply look at the puzzle and decide whether they thought it was possible or impossible. The results were striking. More than 60 percent of unlucky people said that they thought the puzzle was impossible, compared to just 30 percent of lucky people. As in so many areas of their lives, the unlucky people gave up before they even started.

I was also curious to find out how lucky people's expectations influenced their behavior. It seemed possible that if they were convinced that they would perform well at a job interview, they might become overconfident and not find the time to prepare thoroughly. Interestingly, I found no evidence of this at all. Lucky people's expectations about the future did not encourage them to engage in risky behavior. Instead, their positive expectations motivated them to take control of their lives. They attempted to achieve whatever they wanted from life, even if the likelihood of their being successful was quite low.

This simple concept lay behind one of the luckiest breaks of my career. Soon after I started my first job in academia, I received an e-mail that changed my life. The e-mail had been sent out to almost every academic in most British universities. It came from a group of television producers and journalists who wanted to promote science by organizing a huge scientific experiment in which members of the public could participate.

> "Luck is a matter of preparation meeting opportunity."
> —OPRAH WINFREY

The e-mail explained that the experiment would be conducted by BBC television and the *Daily Telegraph* newspaper, and it would reach an audience of more than 18 million people. It asked academics to send in their ideas for the type of experiment that they would like to see carried out. I immediately thought that it would be interesting to conduct a huge study of lie detection. I quickly scribbled down a few notes about how it would be possible to show television viewers a short film of someone either lying or telling the truth, and ask the viewers to telephone and say whether they thought the person was being honest or not. It also occurred to me that it would be interesting to print transcripts of the film in the newspaper and have readers make the same decision. I almost didn't send in my idea because I realized that thousands of academics would submit their proposals and that my idea stood very little chance of being chosen as the winning experiment. Then I thought about it, decided that if I didn't enter, I couldn't win, and so e-mailed my idea to them. A few weeks later I was delighted to discover that my proposal had been chosen.

My experiment was carried out live on BBC television and printed in the *Daily Telegraph*. Thousands of people responded and it was a huge success. Eventually I published the results in one of the world's leading science journals and was invited back year after year to help design and carry out several other large-scale experiments. And it all happened because I decided to submit my original idea, despite thinking that the chances of success were slim.

Luck, Self-Fulfilling Prophecies, and Health

Self-fulfilling prophecies can also have serious implications in another important area of lucky and unlucky people's lives—namely, their physical well-being. The survey described earlier in the chapter showed how many unlucky people expect to experience a wide range of medical problems, including being overweight, suffering from severe insomnia, and having an alcohol problem. Worse still, they are often convinced that they can do nothing to change the situation. They are born unlucky and they believe that unlucky people are destined to lead unhealthy, and unsuccessful, lives. In contrast, lucky people expect to be healthy and well in the future. As in so many areas of their lives, when it comes to health, they expect to be extremely fortunate.

A large amount of research has demonstrated that these types of expectations can have a significant impact on people's well-being.[5] Just as some unlucky people don't take exams because they are convinced that they will fail, or don't bother trying to find jobs because they are certain that they won't get them, so people who are convinced that they will be ill see little point in trying to be healthy. They don't try to stop smoking. They often don't bother to exercise or eat a balanced diet. Neither do they engage in preventative health care or visit a doctor when they feel ill. They are convinced that they are destined to be ill and there is nothing that they can do about the situation.

But what about people with far more positive expectations about the future? It is possible that their high expectations could cause them to engage in risky behaviors. Perhaps they would be so convinced that they would never contract cancer that they wouldn't feel anxious about being a heavy smoker. Or perhaps they would be so certain that they wouldn't catch a sexually transmitted disease that they would take the risk of having unprotected sexual intercourse. Research suggests that nothing could be further from the truth. People with more positive expectations about the future tend to take steps to ensure a healthy lifestyle. They exercise more, eat a balanced diet, take appropriate preventative measures, and pay attention to medical advice.

The impact of these beliefs and behaviors can be far from trivial. Finnish researchers classified more than 2,000 men into three groups—a "negative" group who expected the future to be bleak, a "positive" group who had much higher expectations about the future, and a "neutral" group whose expectations were neither especially positive nor negative. They then monitored the groups over a six-year period and found that the men in the negative group were far more likely to die from cancer, cardiovascular disease, and accidents than those in the neutral group. In contrast, those in the positive group exhibited a far lower mortality rate than those in both the negative and neutral groups.[6]

In Chapter Three we saw how unlucky people have much higher levels of anxiety than neutral and lucky people. These differences can also lead to self-fulfilling prophecies that, in turn, can have a significant effect on lucky and unlucky people's well-being. Research has shown that people who are especially anxious are often very accident-prone, both in their own homes and in the workplace.[7] Anxious people have problems concentrating on what they are doing and are often thinking about their worries and problems rather than about what is happening around them. As a result, it isn't surprising that unlucky people report having many accidents. In addition, other work has shown that such anxiety can affect the body's immune system and can lower defenses against illness. In short, unlucky people's expectations about the future cause them to feel anxious, and these anxieties then cause them to have more than their fair share of accidents and illness. Lucky people are the opposite. They have a far more relaxed attitude toward life and so are far less likely to be accident-prone and to suffer from anxiety-related illnesses.

In addition to having high levels of general anxiety, many unlucky people's beliefs make them especially anxious at certain points in their lives. Recently, an article in the *British Medical Journal* reported that Chinese and Japanese Americans have a 7 percent greater death rate from chronic heart disease on the fourth day of the month. There was no such peak in the deaths of white Americans. Since both Chinese and Japanese regard the number four as unlucky, the researchers concluded that cardiac mortality increases on psychologically stressful occasions. They named the effect after Charles Baskerville, a character in the Arthur Conan Doyle story *The Hound of the Baskervilles*, who suffers a fatal heart attack from extreme psychological stress.[8]

I am not suggesting that lucky and unlucky people's attitude toward their lives completely dictates their well-being—there are some types of disease and illness that are not related to our beliefs and behavior. However, people's expectations about the good and bad fortune that they will experience in the future can have a vitally important impact on many aspects of their health.

Often, lucky people's high expectations also motivate them to persist, even in the face of considerable adversity. At the start of this chapter we met Erik. Erik has achieved many of his lifelong goals, including being in a loving relationship, having a happy family life, and constantly finding work that he has enjoyed. Erik explained the importance he attached to actively trying to make his ambitions a reality:

> You make your own luck through your attitude. If you sit in the house and do nothing then nothing will come to you, but if you're out there working for it then it will come and find you. I firmly believe that I am lucky. Even though things might look a bit bleak at times, I know that it will be all right. As long as you just keep battling away ... as long as you keep on with whatever the problem is, trying to find a way through it for yourself, you'll find the bit of luck that you need will come, and push you through.

Similar views were expressed by many lucky participants, including Marvin, a thirty-three-year-old private detective. Marvin has led an exceptionally lucky life, and has consistently managed to achieve his ambitions even when

the odds were against him. Marvin puts much
of his good luck down to his high expectations
about the future and stressed the importance of
making an effort to achieve whatever it is that
he wants from life:

> I just know that in the end everything
> will be OK. I know that I will win the lot-
> tery. I may not win $10 million, but I know
> that I will get something significant. But
> you do have to try. If you don't buy a ticket
> then you are not going to win. It's the same
> in other aspects of your life. If you expect
> to be lucky, you will be lucky. It's a state of
> mind. My mother and father were a great
> influence on me—I grew up to believe that
> you can do whatever you want if you
> believe in yourself enough and are positive.

Marvin's persistence has certainly paid off.
Despite failing his woodwork exams at school, he
applied for a job as a carpenter in a large ship-
yard. Marvin went to the interview full of energy
and hope. The interviewer was won over by his
enthusiasm and offered him the job. Later on in
his life he decided that he wanted to work as a
private detective. Despite having no formal training or experience, he wrote to all the private
detective agencies in his city. He didn't get even

one reply. Instead of giving up, Marvin put on his best suit and went to visit the offices of one of the largest agencies in his region. The head of the company just happened to be standing in the foyer when Marvin walked in, and the two of them started chatting. The man liked Marvin and offered him a job with the company. A few hours later, Marvin walked away with letterhead stationery, business cards, and his dream job.

I carried out an experiment to examine how lucky and unlucky people's expectations affected how long they would persist in trying to solve a difficult puzzle. The experiment was carried out as part of a television program about my research into luck. I invited lucky and unlucky people to visit my laboratory one at a time. I showed them a huge puzzle that the television company had created especially for the experiment. It consisted of a series of shapes that fit together to make a huge cuboid. I explained that once they left the room, I would dismantle the cuboid. Then, one by one, they would be asked to come into the laboratory to try to reassemble it. They could take as long as they liked on the puzzle, but I didn't tell them that in fact it was almost impossible to solve. I wondered how long each person would persevere before giving up.

The experiment involved three lucky people and three unlucky people. I previously mentioned two of these people—Martin and Brenda—at the end of Chapter Three, because they also took part in the experiment that I carried out to demonstrate how lucky and unlucky people's personalities cause them to create and notice seemingly chance opportunities in their lives. During that experiment, lucky millionaire lottery winner Martin had found the £5 note that we had placed on the street and had struck up a conversation with the successful businessman in the coffee shop. But how would he fare when it came to solving puzzles? Unlucky Brenda had not noticed our £5 note lying on the pavement, nor had she chatted to anyone in the coffee shop. How long would she persevere at the puzzle? Martin and Brenda were joined by four more participants. Unlucky Craig had a reputation for being very accident-prone and encountered nothing but ill fortune whenever he went on vacation. Attractive dancer Sam was unlucky in love. She had dated many men but had yet to find her dream partner. Lucky Bernard was a professional climber who had narrowly escaped avalanches and falls on various mountains around the world, and lucky Peter had twice won large amounts of money on "spot the ball" competitions.

I watched on closed-circuit TV as each person tackled the puzzle. First was lottery winner Martin. Because he was a lucky person, I expected him to persevere for a long time. In fact, he walked into the laboratory, counted the number of blocks, decided that there was one missing, and so said that there was no point in trying to solve the puzzle because it was impossible! Martin's building skills must have been a little rusty, because he miscounted the blocks and was wrong to think that it was impossible. It was a worrying start for my theory. Fortunately, all of the others confirmed my predictions. Unlucky Craig, Sam, and Brenda all gave up after just under twenty minutes, whereas lucky Bernard and Peter continued for much longer. In fact, after half an hour it was quite clear that neither one was even close to quitting. I went into the laboratory and asked them whether they would like to give up. Both of them asked for more time. Eventually I decided to call a halt to their efforts but asked how long they would have continued. Both of them told me that they would have kept going until they had completed the puzzle, regardless of how long it might take.

My research had demonstrated that lucky and unlucky people's expectations were responsible for them achieving, or failing to achieve, many of their ambitions and goals. Unlucky people expected things to go horribly wrong and so often gave up before they began and rarely persisted in the face of failure. Lucky people expected things to work out well and so were much more likely to attempt to achieve their goals, even if the chances of success were slim, and they were far more likely to persevere. These differences actually caused many of the apparently lucky and unlucky events in their lives. Their expectations could make the difference between whether they won or lost competitions, passed or failed important exams, and succeeded or failed to find loving partners.

Subprinciple 3:
Lucky people expect their interactions with others to be lucky and successful.

So far I have described the effect that lucky and unlucky people's extreme expectations about the future have on their thoughts, feelings, and behavior. I have shown how lucky people are more likely to try to achieve their goals and persist longer in the face of failure. But there is one final piece that is needed to complete the puzzle. There is one more type of self-fulfilling prophecy that explains why lucky people frequently obtain what they want from life while unlucky people do not. It is all about the way in which they behave toward other people and how other people respond to them.

The basic idea can again be illustrated with a simple example. Let's imagine that you are going on a blind date. You have agreed to meet a friend of a friend in a restaurant. You don't know the person that you are going to meet, but your friend has told you that your date is likable, friendly, and outgoing. Let's analyze how these expectations might influence your behavior.

Imagine that you walk into the restaurant, find the right table, and sit down opposite your date. A number of things then happen amazingly quickly. First, because you expect your date to be friendly, you are feeling happy, and so you smile. Second, your date sees your smile and correctly assumes that you are pleased to see him. Third, he feels more positively toward you because you seem to feel positively toward him. Fourth, because your date is now feeling positively toward you, he returns your smile. Fifth, you see his smile and this reinforces the notion that he is indeed a friendly person. All of this happens within a few seconds of the two of you meeting, without either of you thinking about it and before anyone has said a single word.

It is a very simple example of how our expectations can cause us to interact with others in a way that makes our expectations a reality. You expected your date to be friendly. This then caused you to smile and lead him to reciprocate your smile and thus appear friendly. It would be easy to imagine how it could all have been very different. Imagine if you had been told that your date had a reputation for being rather unfriendly. If this had been the case you might not have looked forward to the date and not smiled when you first met him. As a result, he would not have smiled at you, thus reinforcing the notion that he was unfriendly. It is a powerful idea. Our expectations about other people influence how we behave toward them and how they respond to us. We do not just have expectations about people, but rather, our expectations can actually cause people to fulfill those expectations. And the effect of these self-fulfilling prophecies extends a long way beyond whether or not we smile when we first meet someone.

Let's analyze a few more minutes of your blind date. After exchanging initial smiles, the two of you start to chat. Beforehand, you were told that your date has a reputation for being very outgoing and extroverted. Once again, your expectations will affect how you interact with him. You might ask if he has been to any good parties recently or if he enjoys talking with people. Once again, your behavior will affect his behavior. These sorts of questions will encourage him to talk about parties and people, and discourage him from telling you that he really loves reading books and spending time on his own. Yet again, your expectations will have increased the likelihood of your date behaving in a way that makes your expectations come true.

Exactly the same idea applies to the different ways in which lucky and unlucky people interact with others. Lucky people expect to meet people who are interesting, happy, and fun to be with. They expect their interactions to go well and be successful. Unlucky people are the opposite. They believe that they are destined to meet people who are far more downbeat, sad, and boring. These very different expectations affect how others respond and, in the long run, play a huge role in dictating how happy and successful lucky and unlucky people will be in their personal and professional lives.

In the workplace, lucky people expect those around them to be productive and competent, and they expect their meetings to be successful and profitable. In contrast, unlucky people do not expect their colleagues and clients to be especially competent or their interactions with them to be especially successful. Research has shown that when it comes to business, these sorts of expectations really matter.

In one study, interviewers were shown job application forms of candidates and asked to rate them as either good or poor. They were then filmed interviewing each candidate. When the interviewers had a high expectation of the candidate, they were very friendly, gave more positive feedback, and sounded cheerful and happy. When they expected the candidate to be less qualified, they were, without realizing it, far less friendly. They gave far less positive feedback and sounded more discouraging. These differences caused the candidates to behave in very different ways. The candidates who interacted with a positive interviewer developed a better rapport with him or her, laughed more, and made a much better impression.[9] In short, the interviewer's expectations affected the way in which the job applicants behaved. Positive expectations helped elicit the best from people, while negative expectations brought out the worst.

> "The luck of having talent is not enough; one must also have a talent for luck."
>
> —HECTOR BERLIOZ

Time and time again, studies have shown that managers' expectations have a profound effect on the productivity of their staff. Managers with high expectations about their subordinates motivate the people around them to perform well, while those with poor expectations cause their staff to become despondent and unproductive. The phenomenon has been found in many different types and levels of business, from life insurance to telecommunications, CEOs to low-level management. Through-out the business world, expectations have the power to become self-fulfilling prophecies.[10]

The effects of these types of self-fulfilling expectations are not limited to business. In another study, men were asked to have a ten-minute telephone conversation with a woman. Beforehand, they were shown one of two photographs and were told that it was a picture of the woman they would be speaking to. One of the pictures showed a very attractive woman while the other showed a very unattractive woman. In fact, all of the men spoke to the same woman. But men who believed that they were talking to an attractive woman were far more outgoing and sociable than those who believed that they were speaking to an unattractive woman. Not only that, their behavior influenced how the woman responded to them. The researchers later played just the woman's half of the conversation to other people and asked them to judge how attractive she was. These people tended to rate the woman as attractive when she had been talking to a man who thought that she was attractive, and unattractive when she had been speaking with a man who thought that she was unattractive. The men's expectations caused them to behave in a certain way, which in turn caused the woman to behave in a way that made the men's expectations come true.[11]

Just as the expectations of the men in the experiment influenced how they spoke to the woman and how she responded to them, so the extreme expectations held by unlucky and lucky people exert a huge influence over their interactions with others.

Take the case of Jill from northern California. Jill is twenty-three and unemployed. She has been unlucky in many aspects of her life but is especially unfortunate when it comes to job interviews:

I've always had bad luck. I've been trying to find a decent job, make a living, and work my way to the top. But the economy is really bad at the moment, so when I first graduated from college, about a year ago, nobody was hiring. During the past year I've been looking really hard. I know that I could be a valuable asset to somebody's company. I know that I'm really smart and have a lot to offer and a lot to say, my interpersonal skills are really good. I went for about twenty-five job interviews, from sales to marketing to PR, but was never offered anything. Sometimes it makes me feel like things are never going to get better, this is just how it is. Because no matter what, things just never seem to go my way. I started to feel really unlucky and became convinced that I would never get a job. It affected how I performed at the interview. I started thinking I don't understand why I'm even here because obviously nobody's gonna hire me. And then I feel like I have to try so much harder than the person who just went in before me. And I get stressed out, and people can read nervousness. I wouldn't say the right things, or maybe the right things were there but they just didn't come out because I was all nerves.

Lucky people are the exact opposite. Many of them described how their high expectations helped them be especially successful in many aspects of their lives. Take the case of Lee. Throughout the book, I have described how Lee is lucky in many areas of his life. He has narrowly escaped several accidents and met his wife quite by chance. But Lee is especially lucky and successful in his job as a sales and marketing manager and has won many awards and accolades. In the previous chapter I described how he puts some of his success down to good intuition. But this is not the full story. He also actively creates high expectations about the future using a technique that he refers to as "dream wishing":

> If I want something, I dream it through. I used to do that in business when I was doing competitions in sales. I would dream that I was winning it and receiving the prize. I'd find myself in bed at night dream wishing. It could be six months ahead to the final outcome, I would still dream it through. I plan telephone calls even before I pick up the receiver. I sit down and I even focus on the person I will be speaking to being positive toward me. Whether I know the person or not, I'd still be thinking and trying to imagine him or her saying the right things to me. At a lot of training courses I mentioned dream wishing and people laughed and probably thought that I was mad! But when I tried it, all of a sudden sales figures started increasing, so I just kept doing it. I've had so many good reactions, and been so successful, that I am certain that there is something to it.

Lee's dream wishing helps him to create positive expectations in his mind about the way that he will interact with others. These expectations often become self-fulfilling prophecies, thus making his goals and ambitions come true.

Lucky people also said that they expected to meet interesting, fun, and attractive people in their personal lives, and they expected their interactions with these people to go well. These expectations can easily become self-fulfilling prophecies. Perhaps the most unusual and compelling example of this came from Andrea, a twenty-five-year-old administrator from Napa in California. In one interview, Andrea described her charmed life:

> It's odd. Things have always worked out for me. It's wonderful because I know that anywhere I go, I can always get a job and a place to live, because it always just happens for me like that. It's given me an amazing amount of confidence and ability to travel. Anywhere I go into I'll be able to get a job. Every job I've ever had, from the first one when I was sixteen, I've just walked in and been hired immediately.
>
> Much of my luck has been concentrated in my love life. I started dating when I was about fifteen years old. I'm OK looking, I'm not an unattractive woman, but somehow I have access to men that by rights I

should have no access to. All I have to do is sit down and talk to somebody, and it can be a man who's completely totally way out of my league, and I just sit down and instantly we start talking. I have dated the cream of the crop, men who were known across the city as fun, powerful, interesting, dynamic guys. I've just gotten engaged, and my fiance is a complete prize.

Andrea obviously seemed to have a magical way of quickly forming strong and positive relationships with the people that she met. I asked her about her expectations when meeting new people. Like many lucky people, she told me that she expected people to be open, friendly, and caring. Unlike many lucky people, these expectations had come about in a rather unusual way:

My father died when I was seven. You'd think that that's the worst thing that can happen to a young girl. And I thought that way for a long time. But when I look back on my father's death now, I realize that it ended up being a strange blessing. All of my teachers felt that they should constantly be nice to me, so I was afforded extra time and help. Any adult that I had to deal with treated me with the utmost kindness and respect. These were my initial impressions of dealing with adults and it's completely colored my life. I expect people to be pleasant and giving. I think it's because I see everybody as really good, at least initially. You'd have to prove yourself otherwise.

The unfortunate loss of her father at an early age had caused Andrea to have a series of positive encounters with adults. These experiences led her to expect the best from the people that she met as an adult, and this, in turn, caused people to respond in a positive way toward her. It is a striking example of how lucky people's expectations can become self-fulfilling prophecies and help them achieve many of their ambitions and dreams.

YOUR LUCK JOURNAL: EXERCISE 11

Your Luck Profile: Principle Three

Remember the Luck Profile that you completed on page xix? Items 6, 7, and 8 on that questionnaire relate to the subprinciples discussed in this chapter. Item 6 asks about the degree to which you expect the future to be bright, Item 7 asks

---

whether you would attempt to get what you want from life when the chances are slim, and Item 8 concerns your attitude toward your interactions with others.

Scoring:

Look back at the ratings you assigned to these three items and then add up those numbers to create a single score (see the following example). This is your score for the third principle of luck.

Statement	Your rating (1–5)
6 I nearly always expect good things to happen to me in the future.	3
7 I tend to try to get what I want from life, even if the chances of success seem slim.	4
8 I expect most of the people that I meet to be pleasant, friendly and helpful.	4
Total for the third principle of luck	11

Now look at the following scale to discover whether your score would be categorized as high, medium, or low. Please make
a note of your score and category in your
Luck Journal, as these results will become
important when we come to discuss how
best to enhance the luck in your life.

Low	Medium	High
3 4 5 6 7 8 9 • 10 11 • 12 13 14 15

⬡

I have asked a large number of lucky,
unlucky, and neutral people to complete
the Luck Profile. Lucky people tend to score
much higher on these items than other
people. Unlucky people tend to obtain the
lowest scores (see the following graph).

Summary

Lucky and unlucky people seem to be living in
different worlds. No matter how hard they try,
unlucky people seem unable to obtain their
goals while lucky people effortlessly achieve
their lifelong dreams and ambitions. My

research has revealed that the two groups of people have very different expectations about the future. Unlucky people are certain that their future will be bleak and that there is nothing they can do about the situation. Lucky people are the complete opposite. They are certain that the future is going to be wonderful and that great things lie in store for them. These unusual and extreme expectations exert a considerable influence over people's thoughts and behavior. They determine whether people try to achieve their goals and how long they persist in the face

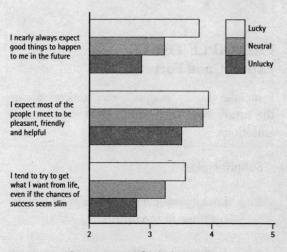

Average scores of unlucky, neutral,
and lucky people on the Luck Profile

of failure. These expectations also determine how they behave toward others and how others respond to them. This reaction, in turn, transforms people's expectations into potent self-fulfilling prophecies that affect their personal and professional lives. Lucky people do not achieve their ambitions by chance. Neither are unlucky people destined never to get what they want from life. Instead, their extreme expectations are responsible for much of their success and failure. Lucky and unlucky people have strong expectations about the future, and these expectations have the power to create that future.

PRINCIPLE THREE:
Expect Good Fortune

Principle: Lucky people's expectations about the future help them fulfill their dreams and ambitions.

Subprinciples:

1.   Lucky people expect their good luck to continue in the future.

2.   Lucky people attempt to achieve their goals, even if their chances of success

seem slim, and persevere in the face of failure.

3.   Lucky people expect their interactions with others to be lucky and successful.

Increasing the Luck in Your Life

The following techniques and exercises will help to raise your expectations about the future and help fulfill your dreams and ambitions. Read through them and think about how you can incorporate them into your daily routine. In Chapter Eight I will describe a systematic program explaining how they can be best used to increase the good fortune in your life.

1. Expect good luck in the future.

Lucky people have very positive expectations about the future. They assume they will be lucky in all areas of their life, and in situations that are both within and outside their control. And these expectations have a major impact on lucky people's lives—they have the power to become self-fulfilling prophecies and make dreams come true. Think back to private detective Marvin and the way his high expectations helped him achieve his dream career. Or Erik, who has been lucky in love and enjoyed all of the many jobs that he has had throughout his life. Erik always thinks positively about the future. If he looks out of the window and sees that it is raining, he thinks, "That's great, my flowers will be out tomorrow." I would like you to spend a little time at the start of each day thinking about the way in which Marvin and Erik create the good luck in their lives. Remember that although lucky people do not take dangerous risks, they do imagine that their future holds nothing but good luck. Convince yourself that your future will be bright and lucky. Set realistic, but high expectations. Take it step by step and see what happens.

SUGGESTED EXERCISES

Affirm Your Luck

Simple affirmations can have a hugely beneficial effect on the way we think and feel. Indeed, many lucky people begin each day by reminding themselves of their good fortune. For the next few weeks I would like you to start each day by repeating the following affirmations to yourself out loud:

"I am a lucky person and today is going to be another lucky day."

"I know that I can be even luckier in the future."

"I deserve good luck and will receive some good fortune today."

At first, you might feel odd. But give it a try and notice the difference.

Set Lucky Goals

This exercise is all about setting your expectations in the right direction by identifying your goals. Write the following three headings on a new page in your Luck Journal:

Short-term goals

Medium-term goals

Long-term goals

Now produce three lists. The first contains your short-term goals—those that you want to attain over the next month. The second list consists of those goals that you want to attain over the next six months. Finally, your list of long-term goals contains your objectives over the next year or more.

Most people find this quite difficult. However, here are a few tips that you might find helpful:

- Think about goals in all aspects of your life—what you would like to achieve on both a personal and professional level.

- Try to make your goals as specific as possible; rather than write a general sentence, such as, "I would like to be happy," try to reflect on the issue and work out what would make you happy—perhaps you would like to be in a loving relationship or have a job that you enjoy. Then try to break these ideas down even further. Perhaps think about the type of partner that you would like to be with, or the type of job that you would find most satisfying. These types of specific goals are far more effective than general goals.

- Most important of all, make your goals achievable. Lucky people have high expectations about the future but do not expect to achieve the impossible. Try to create goals that are attainable. Remember that you can always return to your list and revise it once you have achieved a goal. Take it one step at a time.
- You might find it helpful to jot down a deadline for achieving some of your more important goals. Keep these deadlines realistic and attainable.

This list represents your expectations for the future—the goals that you intend to achieve with your good luck. Look at them on a regular basis and monitor your progress.

2. Attempt to achieve your goals, even if your chances of success seem slim, and persevere in the face of failure.

Earlier on, we saw how unlucky people's expectations sometimes cause them to give up

before they have even started. They don't go on
dates and so never find a partner. They don't
take exams and so are certain to fail. Don't
think like an unlucky person. Instead, let your
lucky expectations about the future motivate
you to try to achieve whatever it is that you
want, even if the chances of your being successful seem quite slim. Also, think back to the
experiment in which I asked people to try to
solve difficult puzzles. The lucky people were
prepared to persevere, even in the face of great
adversity. Think like them. Be open to the idea
of taking a break or trying a different way of
achieving your goals, but be prepared to try, and
try again, until your dreams and ambitions
come true.

SUGGESTED EXERCISE

Carry Out a Cost-Benefit Analysis

Some lucky people acknowledged that
motivating themselves to persevere in the
face of failure is sometimes difficult.
Some said that they carried out the following exercise whenever they felt like
giving up.

First, write down your goal in your Luck Journal. Then draw a vertical line down the center of the page and write the heading "Benefit" at the top of one column and "Costs" at the top of the other.

Now imagine how you might achieve your goal through good luck. Imagine yourself being successful and attaining whatever it is that you really want to happen. As if by magic, your dream has become a reality. In the "Benefit" column, write down all of the benefits that would flow from achieving your goal. Think of everything that you can. How might achieving the goal make you feel better and enrich your personal or professional life? How might it improve your income, add meaning to your life, or help the people that you care about? Keep on adding to the list as you think through the various ways in which you would benefit from achieving your goal.

Next, in the "Costs" column, jot down some of the things that you will have to do to make an effort to attain your goal or carry on persisting. Perhaps you will have to write a few more letters, faxes, and e-mails and make a few more telephone calls.

Perhaps you might have to attend a few more meetings. Perhaps you will have to change some of your habits.

Now take a step back and look at the two lists. Once again, imagine yourself achieving your goal, and compare the costs associated with the benefits. When most people complete this exercise they realize that the benefits far outweigh the costs and find themselves thinking that it is time for action.

3. Expect your interactions with others to be lucky and successful.

Lucky people also have high expectations about their interactions and relationships with others. In their personal lives, they expect the people around them to be interesting, happy, and fun. Remember Andrea? She has led an amazingly lucky life and has always been able to date men that are, in her own words, "the cream of the crop." The secret to Andrea's success has nothing to do with good looks or a large bank balance. Instead, it all comes down to her lucky expectations. She expects the people that she meets to be pleasant, friendly, and helpful. Time and again, her expectations have come true. And the same technique applies in the workplace. Lucky people expect their interactions with colleagues and clients to be both productive and enjoyable. Remember Lee? He is a highly successful sales and marketing manager because of his ability to "dream wish"—he thinks through telephone calls and meetings before they happen and imagines how the people involved will be positive toward him. Once again, his positive expectations have the power to become self-fulfilling prophecies. Try to adopt the same lucky attitude as Andrea and Lee—"dream wish" and expect the best out of the people around you—you might be surprised at the effect that it has on your life.

SUGGESTED EXERCISE

Visualize Good Fortune

During my research, lucky people often spoke about how they visualize themselves experiencing good fortune. Whenever you are faced with an important situation—such as a job interview, meeting, or date—try the following exercise and see what happens.

Find a quiet room and sit in a comfortable chair. Close your eyes and relax. Take a deep breath. In your mind's eye, imagine yourself in the forthcoming situation. Think about the surroundings, the people who will probably be there, the sights and sounds that you are likely to encounter.

Now imagine yourself being lucky and successful in that situation. If you are visualizing a job interview, imagine yourself coming across as competent and knowledgeable. Think about the types of questions that are likely to arise and imagine yourself giving great answers. If you are thinking about a date, imagine yourself being confident and relaxed. If you are about to face a difficult meeting, imagine everyone being friendly and cooperative. Try to visualize the situation in as much detail as possible. Think about what you will be wearing and how you want to behave. Try to anticipate what other people might say and how you would respond. Have fun by trying to see the situation from their point of view and then shifting back to your viewpoint.

Most important of all, focus on how you expect to be lucky and achieve your goals.

Now, slowly open your eyes and make your expectations a reality.

CHAPTER SIX

Principle Four: Turn Bad Luck Into Good

Principle:
Lucky people are able to transform their bad luck into good fortune.

So far, we have explored three principles that lucky people use to create their good luck. But life is not a complete bed of roses for them. Sometimes, even lucky people encounter bad luck and negative events. My research into the way in which they deal with such ill fortune revealed a fourth luck principle: lucky people have an uncanny way of transforming their misfortune into amazing good fortune.

In Japan, there is a common good luck charm

called a Daruma Doll. It is named after a
Buddhist monk who, according to legend, sat so
long in meditation that his arms and legs disap-
peared. The Daruma Doll is egg-shaped with a
heavy, rounded bottom. When you knock it over
it always stands back up. Lucky people are similar to the Daruma Doll. It is not that they never
encounter ill fortune, but rather, when bad luck
happens, lucky people are able to stand straight
back up. My research uncovered why this is the
case. It was like unscrewing the Daruma Doll,
looking inside, and discovering why lucky people
wobble but don't fall down. The secret of lucky
people's ability to turn bad luck into good lies in
four techniques. Together, these form an almost
invincible shield that guards lucky people against
the slings and arrows of outrageous fortune.

Subprinciple 1:
Lucky people see the positive side
of their bad luck.

Have a look at the picture that follows. It shows
two people who appear to be rather unhappy. But
like many things in life, it is all a question of how
you look at it. Turn the book upside down and
look at the picture again. Both the people now

look far happier. The situation hasn't changed, but the way you look at it has. Lucky people use the same approach when they encounter bad luck in their lives. They turn the world upside down and look at things another way.

Imagine being chosen to represent your country in the Olympic Games. You compete in the games, do very well, and win a bronze medal. How happy do you think you would feel? Most of us would, I suspect, be overjoyed and proud of our achievement. Now imagine turning the clock back and competing at the same Olympic Games a second time. This time you do even better and win a silver medal. How happy do you think you would feel now? Most of us think that we would feel happier after winning the silver medal than the bronze. This is not surprising. After all, the medals are a reflection of our performance, and the silver medal indicates a better performance than a bronze medal.

But research suggests that athletes who win bronze medals are actually happier than those who win silver medals. And the reason for this has to do with the way in which the athletes think about their performance. The silver medalists focus on the notion that if they had performed slightly better, then they would have perhaps won a gold medal. In contrast, the bronze medalists focus on the thought that if they had performed slightly worse, then they wouldn't have won anything at all.[1] Psychologists refer to our ability to imagine what might have happened, rather than what actually did happen, as "counterfactual thinking."

YOUR LUCK JOURNAL: EXERCISE 12

Thinking About Bad Luck

Please read each of the following scenarios and imagine that they have actually happened to you. On a new page in your Luck Journal, jot down the degree to which you would rate the scenario as lucky or unlucky using the -3 to +3 scale following each scenario and write a few lines to explain your rating.

Scenario 1: Imagine that you stop suddenly at a traffic light and the car behind you hits the back of your car. Your car is badly damaged and you suffer minor whiplash injuries.

How lucky or unlucky would you rate yourself if this event happened to you?

Very unlucky   Very lucky

\- 3   - 2   - 1   0   + 1   + 2   + 3

Why?

Scenario 2: Imagine that you need a loan from your bank. You arrange a meeting with your bank manager and explain the situation. The manager is clearly in a hurry, and refuses to loan you the full amount of money, but says that he is prepared to lend you half of what you have asked for.

How lucky or unlucky would you rate yourself if this event happened to you?

Very unlucky   Very lucky

\- 3   - 2   - 1   0   + 1   + 2   + 3

Why?

Scenario 3: Imagine losing your wallet containing some cash, your credit cards, and a few personal items of sentimental value. The following day the wallet is handed in to the police and they return it to you. When you look inside the wallet you realize that the cash and credit cards are missing, but the personal items are still there.

How lucky or unlucky would you rate yourself if this event happened to you?

Very unlucky   Very lucky
- 3   - 2   - 1   0   + 1   + 2   + 3

Why?

Scoring:

Look at the ratings that you have assigned to the three scenarios. Unlucky people tend to give two or more negative ratings to the scenarios while lucky people tend to give two or more positive ratings.

Now look at the reasons you have given

to support your ratings. What do they reveal about the way you see the events in your life? Unlucky people tend to concentrate on the negative aspects of the events and write about how the outcome could have been better. Lucky people tend to see the more positive side of things and reflect upon how the outcome could have been much worse.

This chapter explains how these very different ways of looking at the ill fortune in your life is strongly related to your ability to transform bad luck into good.

I wondered whether lucky people might be using counterfactual thinking to soften the emotional impact of the ill fortune that they experienced in their lives.[2] Do they imagine how things could have been even worse whenever they experience bad luck, and therefore feel better about the ill fortune that has happened to them? To find out, I decided to present lucky and unlucky people with some unlucky scenarios and see how they reacted. This work was carried out in collaboration with my research assistant at the time, Matthew Smith, and psychologist Dr. Peter Harris. We looked back over some of the experiences that people had described in their interviews and correspondence, and devised a few simple scenarios.

The first scenario was based on a newspaper article that I came across toward the start of my research. The article described how a man named Ronald had experienced an unusual and unfortunate series of events. A few months before, Ronald had been standing on a railroad platform when a complete stranger came up to him and shot him with an air gun. Ronald tried to restrain the man, and in the ensuing scuffle, the stranger pulled a knife and stabbed him in the face. It was a vicious and totally random attack. Ronald just happened to be in the wrong place at the wrong time. In his letter to me, Ronald described how he thought that he was certainly unlucky to have been attacked, but on the other hand he felt lucky because the air pellet ricocheted off his larynx to the left, and not the right, where it would have badly damaged his vocal cords. We used a simplified version of Ronald's unfortunate experience as the basis for the first scenario in the experiment.

We asked lucky and unlucky people to imagine that they were waiting in line at a bank. Suddenly, an armed robber enters the bank, fires a shot, and the bullet hits them in the arm.

We then asked everyone to rate the degree to which they thought that this would be lucky or unlucky by assigning it a number on the following scale:

Very unlucky						Very lucky
- 3	- 2	- 1	0	+ 1	+ 2	+ 3

The differences between the way in which many lucky and unlucky people responded were amazing.

In the last chapter we met unlucky Clare. She has endured a long string of broken relationships and has never enjoyed any of the many jobs that she has tried. Clare thought that being shot in the arm by a bank robber would be very unlucky, gave it a -3 rating, and commented that it would be just her bad luck to be in the bank during the robbery.

In Chapter Two I described the unlucky life of publisher Stephen. Stephen has been extremely unfortunate when it comes to financial matters—an untrustworthy lawyer almost bankrupted his business and Stephen has frequently missed out on several moneymaking opportunities. Stephen gave the scenario a -2 and noted: "I find this most odd—how can this situation be considered lucky, unless, of course, you enjoy getting shot."

Lucky people viewed the scenario as being far luckier, and often spontaneously commented on how the situation could have been far worse. Throughout this book we have encountered our lucky sales and marketing manager, Lee. Lee is often in the right place at the right time, has good intuition, and uses "dream wishing" to create very lucky expectations about the future. When we asked Lee whether being shot during the robbery would be lucky or unlucky, he immediately said that it would be very lucky and assigned it a rating of +3, He then commented: "The bullet could have killed you outright—if it only hits you in the arm then you may still have a chance."

In the previous chapter I described how lucky private detective Marvin's high expectations about the future have helped him achieve many of his dreams and ambitions. Like Lee, Marvin thought that being shot in the arm by the robber would be very lucky and he also assigned it a +3 rating. His comments also revealed some insight into his lucky life: "It's lucky because you could have been shot in the head—also, you could sell your story to the newspapers and make some money."

In another scenario we asked our subjects to imagine that they had accidentally slipped on some loose stair carpet, fallen down a flight of stairs, and twisted their ankle. Again, everyone was asked to rate the scenario on the same "very unlucky" to "very lucky" scale and, once again, unlucky and lucky people viewed the event in quite different ways. Clare gave the situation a −3.

In contrast, both Lee and Marvin rated the event as being very lucky and awarded it a +3 rating. Both Lee and Marvin said that they would have been lucky to have escaped with just a twisted ankle, as they could have broken their neck or back.

The differences between the lucky and unlucky people were amazing. Many unlucky people saw nothing but misery and despair when they imagined themselves experiencing the bad luck described in the imaginary scenarios. Lucky people were the opposite. They consistently looked on the bright side of each situation and spontaneously imagined how things could have been worse. This made them feel better and helped maintain the notion that they were lucky people living lucky lives.

The different ways in which lucky and unlucky people looked at the ill fortune in their lives emerged in many of my interviews. Agnes, an artist from California, has a very happy family life and has been lucky throughout her career. Agnes has come face to face with death on several occasions throughout her life. When she was five years old, she slipped and fell headfirst into an open fire. When she was seven, the gas pipe next to her house fractured and gas seeped into the room in which she was sleeping. A few years later, she was playing by the sea and almost drowned when she fell into a concealed pothole. When she was in her teens she was hit by a car.

Amazingly, Agnes hasn't let this lifetime of accidents and injury get her down. Instead, her spontaneous ability to imagine how each of the situations could have been much worse has helped keep her spirits high and let her see herself as a lucky person. When she told me about how she had fallen in the fire, she pointed out that her grandfather had put out the fire and thus prevented her from experiencing far greater injuries. When she described inhaling the gas fumes, she said that her habit of sleeping with the blankets over her head had saved her from inhaling lethal amounts of gas. And when she spoke about being hit by the car, she pointed out that it had only just turned around a corner and therefore was traveling fairly slowly. According to Agnes, she was not unlucky to have experienced these accidents, but lucky to have survived them.

Lucky people tend to imagine spontaneously how the bad luck they encounter could have been worse, and in doing so, they feel much better about themselves and their lives. This, in turn, helps keep their expectations about the future high and increases the likelihood of their continuing to live a lucky life. But this use of counterfactual thinking is not the only way in which lucky people imagine that any apparent bad luck could have been even worse. They also compare themselves to other people who have experienced even more ill fortune. The basic idea can be illustrated with the help of a simple optical illusion. Have a look at the following two figures.

Figure 1

Figure 2

The black circle in Figure 1 appears to be larger than the black circle in Figure 2. In fact, the two of them are identical, but they appear to be different sizes because our brains automatically compare each of the circles to their surroundings. The circle on the left is surrounded by small circles and so, in comparison, appears to be relatively large. The circle on the right is surrounded by large circles and therefore appears to be relatively small. The same concept applies when people decide how lucky or unlucky they are.

Imagine that the circles represent the salaries of you and your colleagues in two different jobs. The black circles represent your salary, and the gray circles represent your colleagues' salaries. The circles in Figure 1 represent your first job and the circles in Figure 2 represent your second job. In both jobs you are earning the same amount of money, as shown by the fact that the two black circles are the same size. However, psychologically, it won't feel like that. In the first job you are earning more than your colleagues and so, psychologically, you are likely to feel more satisfied with the situation. In the second job they are earning more than you, and so, psychologically, you are likely to feel more dissatisfied with the situation.

When it comes to looking at the bad luck in their lives, lucky and unlucky people often engage in this type of comparative thinking. In the previous section I described how unlucky Clare always looked on the negative side of the unlucky imaginary scenarios that I presented to her. In addition, she also tended to magnify the impact of her bad luck by comparing herself to people who appeared luckier than her. In one interview, she told me why she felt unlucky in her current job:

> If anything goes wrong at work it always seems to be me, never anybody else. I keep seeing people at work having luck, buying new cars, having vacations, going out to clubs, getting time off work—and I can't afford vacations and I keep thinking "Why me?"

In contrast, lucky people tend to lessen the impact of their ill fortune by comparing themselves to people who have been unluckier than themselves. An especially compelling example of this emerged when I spoke to participant Mina. Mina grew up in Poland during the early part of World War II. The occupying forces frequently rounded up large groups of people in the street and transported them to prisons and concentration camps. One day, Mina narrowly escaped being rounded up by quickly hiding in a small courtyard. Unfortunately, many of her friends and family were not so lucky. Not surprisingly, these events have remained with her throughout her life and still affect how she views any ill fortune that she encounters:

Whenever anything bad happens I think about the people who were, or are, much worse off than me—the people who were taken to the concentration camps, or who were disabled by the war—I might think I am unlucky in this and that for a while, but then I think of all those people and the really horrendous situations they had to endure, and I realize that I am so much better off.

In short, lucky people soften the emotional impact of any bad luck that they have encountered by imagining how the situation could be even worse and by comparing themselves to people who have experienced far greater ill fortune than they have experienced.

Subprinciple 2:
Lucky people are convinced that any ill fortune in their lives will, in the long run, work out for the best.

There is also a second vitally important technique that underlies lucky people's ability to transform bad luck into good—and the thinking behind this one dates back thousands of years.

There is an ancient parable about a wise farmer who realized that many of the seemingly unlucky events in our lives often have an uncanny way of turning out to be lucky in the long run. One day, the farmer was out riding when his horse suddenly threw him to the ground. The farmer landed badly and broke his leg. A few days later his neighbor came to commiserate with him on his bad luck, but the farmer replied, "How do you know that this is bad luck?" A week later, people in the village were due to hold a special festival, but the farmer was unable to attend the celebrations because of his broken leg. Once again, his neighbor expressed some sympathy for his misfortune and, once again, the farmer replied, "How do you know that this is bad luck?" There was a terrible fire at the festival and many people died. The neighbor realized that the farmer's run of apparent ill fortune had helped save his life, and that the farmer had been right to question whether these events had been unlucky.

Many lucky people share the farmer's attitude toward the bad luck that they encounter. When they look back on their lives they often focus their attention on the benefits that flowed from their ill fortune. In Chapter Three we met lucky Joseph, a thirty-five-year-old mature student who has experienced more than his fair share of life-changing chance opportunities. Joseph also has an amazing ability to create good fortune from his bad luck. Joseph is now studying for a psychology degree and leads a happy and law-abiding life. When he was younger, life was very different. He was in constant trouble with the police and, on one occasion, was arrested while trying to break into an office building and was sent to jail. Looking back, Joseph now thinks that this was one of the luckiest things that ever happened to him:

In my twenties I was hanging around with two other guys committing lots of small crimes and burglaries. One night we decided to break into an office building. I climbed up onto the roof and, I don't know why, but I had this sudden fear of heights. The alarm bells went off and the other two ran away, but I just couldn't move. The next thing I know, the police arrived and caught me. I went to court and was given four months in prison. While in prison, I found out that my two friends went out to pull another job and were mistaken for some other punks that had a reputation for carrying guns. The police thought my friends were armed and shot at them. One of my friends was shot and seriously wounded—he is now permanently in a wheelchair—and the other was shot dead. Being put in prison was probably the luckiest thing that ever happened to me.

Interestingly, I have often experienced a similar phenomenon. In fact, when I was performing as a magician, one of the unluckiest things to ever happen to me brought me a huge amount of good fortune in the long run. I had been invited over to California to perform at a very prestigious club for magicians—the Magic Castle in Hollywood—and was keen to impress. On the way over, I decided to stop off for a few days in New York. At the time, my entire act fit into a small case, which for obvious reasons, I always kept by my side. At one point I decided to get a snack in a fast-food restaurant and put my case on the chair next to me. A short while later there was a disturbance over on one side of the restaurant and I looked across to see what was happening. When I looked back, I realized that my case had been stolen. It had my entire act inside and I was only a few days away from performing. Worse still, many of the items were simply irreplaceable, and so I quickly had to think about changing my entire act. I went to a local store, bought a few decks of cards, and returned to my hotel room. That night I found out the true meaning of the phrase "Necessity is the mother of invention." I worked into the early hours, figuring out new tricks using the materials that I had at hand. Eventually, I rehearsed several items that I hadn't performed for years and actually invented two tricks. My new act was far better than my original act and the two tricks that I invented were eventually awarded prizes for originality from my fellow performers. I would never have bothered taking the time and trouble to create the tricks if my bag hadn't been stolen. Although I didn't realize it at the time, the theft was one of the luckiest things that ever happened to me when I was performing as a magician.

Lucky people use this concept to soften the emotional impact of the ill fortune in their lives. By looking back and focusing on the positive things that resulted from their apparent bad luck in the past, they feel better about themselves and the future. If bad luck happens to them, they take the long view and expect things to work out well in the end.

Subprinciple 3:
Lucky people do not dwell
on their ill fortune.

Unlucky people tend to dwell on the bad luck in their lives. As one unlucky person put it:

It's almost as though I have had a curse put on me. There have been times when I

don't know where to turn. I have lost a lot
of sleep worrying about everything that
has gone wrong, even though I can't do
anything about it. I wonder what I have
done that is so bad to deserve this.

Lucky people do the opposite. They let go of
the past and focus on the future. In Chapter Four
we found out how meditation helps Jonathan
enhance his intuitive abilities and increase the
good luck that he experiences in his private and
professional life. Jonathan also has a reputation
for being able to transform bad luck into good:

One thing my boss has intimated more
than once is that I always seem to fall on
my feet. Sometimes things don't go all
that well, but somehow I bounce back and
things work out for me.

Interestingly, Jonathan also spoke about how
meditation had helped him let go of some of the
unlucky events that had happened in his life:

I think meditation helps me to get a better
perspective on life. You can switch off, calm
down, and when you wake up destressed, you
take a different view on things. It makes you
realize that if you can't change a situation

then there's no point in getting stressed. If you can take some action and do something about it, then do it. But if there's nothing you can do—like if you're stuck in traffic on the highway—then you might as well forget about it and calm down. Generally, I'm reasonably good at having the ability to just walk away from it. I'm not naturally a brooding person. Most of the time, somehow, I tend to get what I want, but if I don't, I wake up the next day and somehow compartmentalize it. I think "OK, I can't do anything about it and there's no point in thinking about it." Then I just get on with life.

Jonathan wasn't the only one to remark on the importance of letting go. Linda has led a lucky life and has fulfilled many of her dreams and ambitions. I also asked her about how she dealt with any bad luck that she encountered— once again she mentioned the important role that meditation played in forgetting the unlucky events in her past:

I used to go to Buddhist meditation and that was really helpful. I learned to just let things go if they weren't right or bothering me. You just have to put it behind you as an experience that hasn't been good and then try not to worry about it. I find that very easy to do, I don't dwell on stuff.

Seth is a lawyer from New York. He has noticed that much of the good luck in his life is a direct result of apparent ill fortune. When he was a young child he was overweight and was often teased about his size. As a young man he joined Weight Watchers. When he went to his first meeting he met his perfect partner. They attended meetings together for a year, were married a few years later, and have been together ever since. This was not the only example of Seth's ability to survive and even thrive on bad luck:

Looking back, much of the bad luck in my life has been a positive learning experience. Sometimes the learning is just that I can get through life without something that I thought was vitally important. The last few years we've had a very negative stock market. I made some very bad decisions and lost about two million dollars. And I thought that was going to be devastating. But the fact is that it really was something that I could withstand, it wasn't the end of the world. It helped me to put into perspective what that money meant in my life. I still had my job, my health, my family, and my wife.

I very rarely worry about the past. Instead, I look for the treasure in the mountain of trash and very rarely get bogged down with the negative aspects of things. I normally focus on what's good about this situation and how can I benefit from it.

These very different approaches to bad luck have a huge impact on lucky and unlucky people's subsequent thoughts and feelings. Research has shown that when people dwell on the negative events in their lives they start to feel sad. When people concentrate on positive events from their past, they feel much happier. It is not just a case of memory affecting mood. Mood also affects memory. In one very cleverly conceived experiment, psychologists James Laird and his colleagues from Clark University studied the effects of mood on memory.[3] They asked people to read two short passages. The first was a very sad newspaper editorial about the unnecessary killing of dolphins during tuna fishing, and the second was a funny short story by Woody Allen.

The experimenters then used an ingenious technique to make people feel happy or sad. They asked half of the people to hold a pencil between their teeth, but to ensure that it did not touch their lips. Without the people realizing it, the lower part of their faces was forced into a smile. The other half were asked to support the end of the pencil with just their lips and not their teeth. Without them realizing it, this forced the lower part of their faces into a frown. When people force their faces into a smile they actually feel happy. Likewise, when they force their faces to frown they feel sad. Everyone was then given another pencil and asked to write down everything they could remember from the two passages. The results were remarkable. The people who had been forced to smile remembered lots of information from the Woody Allen story and less from the serious editorial. Those who had been forced to frown remembered little about the Woody Allen story and lots more from the editorial. Their mood had affected the information that they remembered. In exactly the same way, when we look back on our lives in a happy mood, we tend to remember life events that worked out well. When we look back in an unhappy mood, we tend to dwell on more negative events that have happened to us.

The two-way relationship between mood and memory explains why lucky people's reluctance to dwell on any ill fortune in their past helps maintain their lucky perspective on life. When unlucky people ruminate on the bad luck that they have encountered, they feel even more unlucky and sad. This, in turn, makes them think more about the ill fortune in their lives and, as a result, feel even more unlucky and sad. So the downward spiral continues, plunging them further and further into an unlucky worldview. Their memories affect their mood, which then affects their memories.

Lucky people are able to avoid this process by being able to forget about the unlucky events that have happened to them and instead focus on their good luck. Their positive memories then make them feel happy and lucky and this, in turn, causes them to think about other times when things worked out well for them. Instead of spiraling downward, they find their memories and moods work together to make them feel luckier and luckier.

YOUR LUCK JOURNAL: EXERCISE 13

Attitudes Toward Ill Fortune

This exercise is all about how you respond when you encounter problems and failure in your life. On a new page in your Luck Journal please give an honest account of how you would respond if the following events happened to you.

Please do not write down what you

would like to believe that you would think and do. Instead, spend a few minutes imagining that the event has actually happened and then give an honest description of how you think you would actually respond.

Event 1: You take your driving test four times but fail each time. How would you respond if this happened to you?

Event 2: You have applied for a promotion at work each year for the past three years, but have been turned down each time. How would you respond if this happened to you?

Event 3: You have made three attempts to mend a dripping pipe in your ceiling and each time you have made the situation worse. How would you respond if this happened to you?

Interpretation:

I have asked many lucky, unlucky, and neutral people these questions. Their answers tend to include the following elements.

Unlucky people tend to describe how they would simply give up and learn to live with the problem, would not consider trying to discover why they had been unsuccessful in the past, and would consider ineffective forms of problem solving, such as relying on superstition.

Lucky people are the opposite. They tend to describe how they would persevere rather than give up, how they would treat these kinds of experiences as opportunities to learn from past mistakes, and how they would explore novel and more constructive ways of solving the problem, such as consulting experts and engaging in lateral thinking.

Subprinciple 4:
Lucky people take constructive steps to prevent more bad luck in the future.

Imagine that you have gone on three dates, but each one ended in failure. Or you have had four job interviews but were rejected each time.

Or you went shopping to buy an item of clothing, found exactly what you wanted, but then discovered that there were long lines at the checkout. How would you respond in each of these situations? Would you persist or give up? Carry on or break down? I put these sorts of scenarios and questions to many of the lucky and unlucky people involved in my research. I wanted to discover how the two groups of people would behave in the face of ill fortune. I asked everyone to describe how they felt about the situations and, more important, what they would do next. The results revealed a fascinating insight into the psychology of luck.

In the previous chapter, I described how lucky and unlucky people's expectations were related to how much they persevered in the face of adversity. Unlucky people were convinced that they were going to fail and so often didn't bother to try very hard. Lucky people were the opposite. They were sure of success and so were happy to persevere. Exactly the same difference emerged when I asked the two groups of people how they would respond to ill fortune. The unlucky people often said that they would simply give up. After imagining that three of their dates had ended in failure, one unlucky person commented:

I wouldn't do anything. I suppose I'd

just think that's the way it's meant to be, if those three dates don't work out, then I wouldn't pursue anything after that.

When they imagined finding their perfect item of clothing, only to discover long lines at the checkout, they commented:

I would probably cry for a week and just forget it, or I'd wait in the line, knowing that when I got to the end of the line the cash register would break down and that would be that. Then I'd have a tantrum.

The lucky people were far more persistent. In their minds they were convinced that they were not destined to be unlucky. Instead, they saw ill fortune as a challenge that needed to be overcome; it could lead to better luck in the future. After imagining going on three failed dates, one lucky person explained how she would persevere:

I'd try, try, and try again. Don't be deterred, go for it. You can't just give up that easy. Life's set these little tasks for you and you've just got to see them through.

After imagining failing three job interviews, another wrote:

I'd just shrug my shoulders and carry on. I'd just immediately write to more places. I think probably the same day I'd write off to more places, so I felt that I was doing something positive.

The lucky and unlucky people's responses to my questions revealed another important difference. Lucky people approached the unlucky situations in a far more constructive way than unlucky people. Unlucky people hardly ever spoke about trying to discover why they had not been successful in the past. They were reluctant to learn from their mistakes and so were far more likely to repeat them in the future. In contrast, lucky people often spontaneously said that they would treat their failures as an opportunity to learn and grow. When it came to the three failed dates, one lucky person said:"I would try to improve my luck by listening to the third date to see where my faults were ... if there were any."

Another lucky person adopted the same approach when describing how he would respond to three failed job interviews: "I would probably write to the interviewer and ask them where I went wrong, I would ask them for some feedback and then make sure whatever I did wrong was corrected for the next interview."

So, lucky people persist and have more constructive responses in the face of failure. In this way, they can turn bad luck into good. But lucky people also often mentioned a third type of response to the events. This can perhaps be best illustrated with the following puzzle. Imagine that I give you a candle, a box of thumbtacks, and a book of matches. It is your job to affix the candle to the wall in such a way that it can be lit and used as a light. Some people stick the thumbtacks in the wall and try to balance the candle on the pins. Others try to melt the bottom of the candle with the matches and then try to stick the candle to the wall. Neither of these approaches works. In fact, only a small number of people come up with the correct solution. These people empty the thumbtacks from the box, and then use two of the thumbtacks to attach the box to the wall. It is then easy to place the candle on the box and light it. It is a simple, elegant, and effective solution. It is also one that requires creativity and flexible thinking. It requires people to see the objects that they have been given in a rather lateral way. To them, the box containing the thumbtacks isn't just a box—it could also be a candleholder. They found a solution because of their unusual way of approaching the problem. They were successful because of their ability to think outside the box about the box.

My research revealed that lucky people used

the same approach when they tackled the bad-luck scenarios in my experiment. When ill fortune blocked the path to their goals, they explored other ways of solving the problem. After imagining three failed dates, one lucky person remarked:

> I think I'd probably just give men a rest for a while and do something with my girl-friends, or just people who were friends, and just not push it. Just sit back and let it happen a bit more naturally rather than date, date, date with different people.

Another spontaneously suggested that he would try to overcome the lines at the check-outs in a rather novel way:

> ... sometimes you can just walk up to the cashier and say, "Can you put this on hold until tomorrow, and I'll come and get it then." Sometimes they will do it.

The unlucky people rarely came up with these type of ideas. When bad luck blocked their chosen road, they tended to go back home rather than look for an alternative route. In fact, only one unlucky person produced one response that was in any way creative or novel. And, interestingly, this involved his eliminating the problem by changing what he wanted out of life, as opposed to overcoming the bad luck that had happened to him. When I asked this man how he would respond to three failed dates, he thought about the question for a while, then suddenly looked up, smiled, and said that he would probably become a priest.

Exactly the same factors spontaneously emerged in my interviews with lucky and unlucky people about the ill fortune in their actual lives. Unlucky people often didn't try to learn from past mistakes or explore novel ways of tackling their ill fortune. Instead, they were convinced that they couldn't change the situation and just endured it.

Take the case of Shelly, a nurse. She had a very happy childhood and eventually became a student nurse at a well-known teaching hospital. After passing her exams, she traveled all around the world and lived a rather charmed life. Then, quite by chance, she met her husband, Paul. He had been very unlucky in his life, and Shelly believes that his bad luck rubbed off on her. The rest of her life has been plagued by health problems, unemployment, and unhappiness.

Shelly bought her first car in 1983. Unfortunately, her husband died a few weeks later, and shortly after the funeral, she experi-

enced her first car accident. The trauma of her
husband's death, combined with that of the
accident, resulted in a four-week memory loss,
and so Shelly's recollection of the accident is
somewhat vague. But she is certain that it was
not her fault; it was instead due to the car being
jinxed. She does, however, have very clear memories of what happened when she bought her
second car. Shelly takes up the story here:

> The first accident I had was when the car
> in front of me suddenly, and without warn-
> ing, turned left and removed my headlight.
> I took the blame because the law says that I
> must have been too close. Next, I hit the car
> in front of me when it braked sharply.
> Accident number three was when I went
> down a railway embankment. I don't know
> why that happened. I simply went to pick
> something up from the passenger's seat,
> and the car went off the road and hit a wall.
> After that, it demolished some traffic lights.
> I had had enough. I got rid of it.

These experiences might have caused most
people to question their driving skills. The accidents happened in three different cars and Shelly
was often seen to have been at fault. But Shelly is
adamant that the accidents were due to her bad

luck and three jinxed cars. As a result, she is convinced that there is very little she can do about
the problem. It is just the way things are.

Even when unlucky people do try to change
their bad luck, they often engage in behaviors
that are far from constructive. Instead of trying
to improve her driving skills, Shelly tried to
change her bad luck by helping others:

> There are many times when disaster
> strikes whatever you do—or it often does-
> n't seem to know when to stop. It is as
> though whatever forces cause these things
> have your name and that is that. I thought
> I was being punished and tried to make
> amends. I cared for my sick and aged
> mother for years, rescued animals, and
> did my bit for charity. No matter how I
> tried, nothing has gone right. I catalogued
> events in diaries for several years, waiting
> to see when the tide would turn. It never
> did and I threw them away.

Shelly is not the only unlucky person to have
tried, and failed, to change her bad luck. In
Chapter Five I described the unlucky life of
Clare. She has had a great deal of ill health, dis-
liked all of the jobs that she has tried, and has
been very unlucky in love. In one interview, I

asked her whether she had tried anything to decrease the bad luck in her life. She explained how she had relied upon superstition:

> Three or four months ago I got a letter from a clairvoyant offering to help. It said things like I hadn't had a very happy childhood, and I was thinking "Well, how does she know that?" Thinking about it now, I guess it was probably just a standard letter that would fit somebody eventually. Anyway, I fell for it and sent her some money—$50—and she sent me all these numbers to pick for the lottery, but of course they were no good. She told me that these would bring me untold wealth. I did use them—in fact I'm still using them at the moment. But so far they've not been any good and I have won nothing.

This type of superstitious behavior is fairly harmless. However, some of my other interviews revealed that superstitious thinking had had a far more dramatic, and negative, impact on the lives of unlucky people.

Take the case of Paul, a seventy-five-year-old retired salesman. In his teens Paul became very interested in superstition and came across an old book on astrology that informed him that his lucky number was three. Paul decided to put the idea to the test. He visited a local racecourse in Florida, looked down the lists of horses that would be running that day, and placed bets on several horses that were listed third in each race. Paul told me what happened next:

> To my total amazement, three of the horses won and I walked away with a large amount of money—the equivalent to more than a year of my wages. At the time, I thought that I was the luckiest person alive. Looking back, I now think that this was the unluckiest day of my life. In those days I was pretty superstitious and I became convinced that three really was my lucky number.

For the next few weeks Paul placed a large number of bets on horses listed third on several race cards. When the horses failed to win, Paul switched his attention to dog racing. He visited dog tracks night after night and placed bets on every third dog listed in every third race. In just one month, Paul lost all of his original winnings. But instead of learning from his mistakes, Paul continued to rely on superstition and still placed large bets on horses and dogs listed third on race cards. He continued to lose large sums of money

at the racetracks and had to find ways of trying
to cover the costs of his debts. Eventually, his
furniture was repossessed, and Paul and his
family were evicted for nonpayment of rent.
Many years later, Paul is able to look back on his
life and see the way in which his superstitious
thinking was at the root of his bad luck—he still
continues to gamble, but now he relies on judg-
ment rather than lucky numbers.

Intrigued by these interviews, I carried out a
systematic survey of the superstitious beliefs
held by the people involved in my research. I
wanted to learn if superstition affected unlucky
people more than lucky people. I asked all the

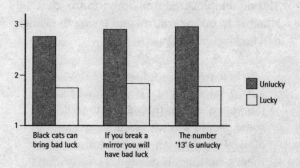

Average scores of unlucky and lucky people on the three
questions concerning well-known superstitions

participants to indicate on a scale from 1 (disagree) to 7 (agree) whether they thought that
the number thirteen was unlucky, whether they
felt uneasy when they broke a mirror, and
whether they would expect a black cat crossing
their path to make them experience ill fortune.
The results showed that unlucky people were
far more superstitious than lucky people[*] and
provided more evidence to support the notion
that unlucky people tended to rely on ineffective ways of trying to alter the bad luck that they
encountered in their lives.

My interviews also provided further evidence
that lucky people take a far more constructive
approach when they try to change their ill fortune. Earlier on, I described the lucky life of private detective Marvin. Like many lucky people,
Marvin emphasized the importance that he
attaches to taking control and trying to change
bad luck when it happens:

When people say that they hate their
jobs, I say to them, "If you don't like the
job you're doing, then get out of it." But
some people will say,"Well, I can't get out
of it, I'm stuck in it, I'm unlucky and
there's nothing else." But I really don't
believe in that way of thinking. I believe if
you're not happy in what you do, then you

should actively look to change it. Because if you change what you do to something you enjoy doing, you'll feel better about yourself and change your luck as well.

Hilary, age forty-six, is a physician from Berkeley, California. She has experienced a great deal of ill fortune in her life but considers herself very lucky:

It hasn't been like I find lucky pennies on the street or win lotteries. It's more that the really important aspects of my life have always worked out well. And I have noticed that, with very few exceptions, the bad things that have happened to me have always turned out for the best.

Despite a difficult childhood, I tend to be very proactive and do not ascribe events to bad luck. I definitely take an active role in my life. I take action rather than watch things go off-course. Those difficult childhood years also made me quite determined to get what I want out of life.

After I graduated from medical school, I was accepted for residencies at Stanford, Yale, and Johns Hopkins.

In 1984 I finished my residency, and I signed a contract to work as a pathologist

with a small hospital. About a week before
I was set to start, I sold most of my furniture and had the rest transported to my
new home. Then I got a call from the hospital director saying that they had been
sold to a giant corporation and that the
contract that I had signed was void because
they no longer had control of the hospital.
So I had no contract and no job. I was very
upset. Then I noticed that a hospital in the
Bay Area was actively recruiting for someone to work in a new but rapidly develop-
ing area of medicine. I had never thought
of switching fields, but I applied and was
offered the position. Now I couldn't see
myself doing anything else. I know in ret-
rospect that I really was not cut out to be a
pathologist, and that I would have been
miserable if I had followed that career path.
So something that was fairly disastrous
turned into something wonderful.

Many of the interviews also supported the
notion that lucky people explore novel ways of
solving the problems in their lives. In Chapter
Four, I described how Jonathan used meditation to promote his intuition in the workplace.
Earlier on in this chapter, I noted that he also
had a reputation for being able to transform

bad luck into good, and was able to let go of any unlucky things that happened to him. When I interviewed Jonathan, he told me about how he persisted in the face of failure and enjoyed trying to find novel solutions to problems:

My German grandfather had a phrase which, loosely translated, means, "For our family, it comes difficult, but it does come eventually." I always tell the kids never to give up, you have to struggle, but it will happen. I think my grandfather's attitude has remained with me—if there is even a one percent chance, I'll normally continue. I am also quite flexible. I wouldn't regard myself as a creative person in the usual way—I'm not naturally creative musically or artistically. But I've made a deliberate point of trying to think laterally and not think on the straight and narrow. I love the challenge of being focused but trying to find an unusual way round to find that solution, not necessarily the straight way.

Lucky people take a far more constructive approach to the ill fortune in their lives. They take action, persist, and consider alternative solutions. All of this helps them minimize the chances of experiencing more bad luck in the future.

Emily's Story

Perhaps the most compelling example of how bad luck can be turned into good came from Emily. Emily is forty years old, was originally from British Columbia, and now works at a publishing company in Pennsylvania. Emily is convinced that much of her good luck has grown out of some of the unluckiest events in her life.

When I was a young girl, my parents forced me to go to a girls' group, like the Girl Scouts. Meetings were held at the local church hall and there was this wall that was about thirty-five feet high and easy to climb. I decided to show off and climb the wall. Just as I got to the top, I started to hear the nails coming out of the wall. It was like a horror film, four nails came out and I was thrown to the ground. I could have been killed, but instead only ripped my foot apart. I didn't walk for six months, but at least I didn't die.

When Emily was thirty-two, she was working at an art gallery in British Columbia. One night, she was bicycling home late and rode up a back alley. A car with no headlights on came out of the darkness and drove directly toward her. The car hit the front wheel of her bike, flipping it over, ran over Emily's head, and drove away. Emily suffered considerable head injuries, but once more turned her bad luck into good:

In British Columbia the government runs car insurance, so I was able to sue, even though I didn't get the license plate number of the driver. I was awarded thirty thousand Canadian dollars. This allowed me to make some positive changes in my life that I had been considering for a while. I left Canada and went to the United States, and managed to find work in the publishing industry. So out of that extreme near-death experience, it turned into a new life, rather like a phoenix rising.

This pattern of events has occurred time and again in Emily's life. She is unfortunate enough to encounter bad luck, but her attitude and behavior toward her ill fortune has allowed her to transform her experiences into good luck:

Last spring I blew out my kneecap, but had no medical coverage. I could barely walk and was on a cane for five months. Everybody's like, "Oh my God, and you live in a three-story walk-up!" I'm like, "That's OK, I could really do with sitting around and slowing down for a few months, this is fine. Wanna come over and watch a movie?" Instead of bemoaning the fact that I can't go dancing or biking, I enjoy whatever I have to work with.

I have ways of coping with my bad luck. I think, well, I can lie here and dwell on the problem, or I can think about what I can do to positively affect whatever fortune has handed me. And in years gone by, my anxiety about the bad luck in my life would wake me up, and it would be vomiting, nausea, lack of sleep. Then I would be completely ineffectual the next day. But for me it's now a training process. When I wake up in a blind sweat panic, I just think, "There is nothing you can do at four o'clock in the morning, nothing you do right now is going to positively affect what you need done. So breathe it out and go to sleep. Just let it go."

Some of the greatest things that have happened to me have come out of the worst things. And as I get older I am taking fewer chances—I am not as prone to throwing myself out into the thrall of the universe. But I've been worried that if I don't keep my spirit of adventure going, perhaps I will lose the bonus perks that come from it. So I'm trying to find a happy medium of experiment and adventure and taking the right kind of chances.

Luck is what it is. People call things good luck or bad luck, but to me luck is just what it is. It's your choice to see the good or the bad.

YOUR LUCK JOURNAL: EXERCISE 14

Your Luck Profile: Principle Four

It is time to return to the Luck Profile that you completed on page xix. Items 9, 10, 11, and 12 on this questionnaire relate to the subprinciples discussed in this chapter. Item 9 asks about the degree to which you look at the positive aspects of events in your life, Item 10 asks whether you take the long view of any apparent ill fortune, Item 11 concerns the degree to which you dwell on your past failures, and Item 12 examines the degree to which you try to learn from bad luck in the past.

Scoring:

Look back at the ratings that you assigned to these four items and then add up those numbers to create a single score (see the following example). This is your score for the fourth principle of luck.

Statement	Your rating (1–5)
9 I tend to look on the bright side of whatever happens to me.	5
10 I believe that even negative events will work out well for me in the long run.	4
11 I don't tend to dwell on the things that haven't worked out well for me in the past.	5
12 I try to learn from the mistakes that I have made in the past.	4
Total for the fourth principle of luck	**18**

Now look at the following scale to discover whether your score would be categorized as high, medium, or low. Please make a note of your score and category in your Luck Journal, as these results will become important when we come to discuss how best to enhance the luck in your life.

Low	Medium	High
4 5 6 7 8 9 10 •	11 12 13 14 15 16 •	17 18 19 20

⬡

I have asked a large number of lucky, unlucky, and neutral people to complete the Luck Profile. Lucky people tend to score much higher on these items than other people. Unlucky people tend to obtain the lowest scores (see the following graph).

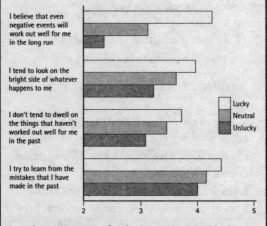

Average score of unlucky, neutral, and lucky people on the Luck Profile

Summary

Lucky people are not born with a magical ability to turn bad luck into good. Instead, often without realizing it, they employ four psychological techniques to overcome, and even thrive upon, the ill fortune in their lives. First, lucky people imagine how things could have been worse and they compare themselves to people who are unluckier than themselves. Second, they take the long view and assume that something positive will come from their bad luck. Third, they do not dwell on the ill fortune that they have encountered. Fourth, they assume that there is something they can do about their ill fortune—they persist, think about lateral ways around the problem, and learn from their mistakes. Together, these techniques explain their uncanny ability to cope with, and often even thrive upon, any ill fortune that comes their way.

PRINCIPLE FOUR:
Turn Bad Luck Into Good

Principle: Lucky people are able to transform their bad luck into good fortune.

Subprinciples

1. Lucky people see the positive side of their bad luck.

2. Lucky people are convinced that any ill fortune in their lives will, in the long run, work out for the best.

3. Lucky people do not dwell on their ill fortune.

4. Lucky people take constructive steps to prevent more bad luck in the future.

Increasing the Luck in Your Life

The following techniques and exercises will help transform your bad luck into good fortune. Read through them and think about how you can incorporate them into your daily routine. In Chapter Eight I will describe a systematic program explaining how they can be best used to increase the good fortune in your life.

1. Look on the positive side of your bad luck.

Lucky people tend to see the positive side of

their ill fortune. They imagine how things could have been worse. Remember how Marvin thought that falling down the stairs and twisting his ankle was really lucky, because he thought about how he could have broken his neck? Lucky people also compare themselves to people who are unluckier than themselves. Remember Mina, who softens the impact of the ill fortune in her life by comparing herself to the people that she saw experiencing terrible events during World War II? Try to think like Marvin and Mina, and look on the bright side of whatever happens to you.

SUGGESTED EXERCISE

Find the Treasure in the Trash

I asked lucky people to describe the sorts of techniques that they used to see the positive side of any ill fortune that comes their way. Here are the three ideas that were mentioned most often.

- Think of ways in which the situation could have been far worse. You may have experienced a car accident, but at least you survived. You may have been late for an important appointment, but then again, you could have missed it altogether.

- Ask yourself if the unlucky event really matters. You may have been turned down for a promotion, but will that affect the important aspects of your life, such as your health and your relationships with others? You may have lost your wallet and credit cards, but does that really matter in the overall scheme of your life?

- Compare yourself to those who are less fortunate. You may have a bad back, but there are many people in the world suffering from far more serious illnesses. Compared to them, your bad luck is trivial.

Whenever bad luck strikes, use these techniques to make yourself feel better about your situation.

2. *Remember that the ill fortune in your life may work out for the best.*

Lucky people also take the long view—if bad luck happens to them, they expect things to work out well in the end. Remember how lucky Joseph described how being sent to prison was one of the best things that ever happened to him? Think like Joseph—take the long view and remember that any ill fortune may work out for the best.

SUGGESTED EXERCISE

Create a Phoenix From the Ashes

Many people who have faced terrible life events say that, in the long run, the event helped them re-evaluate their lives and realize the importance of the things that really mattered to them, such as their family and friends. When bad things happen, spend a few moments thinking about the good luck that might flow from your ill fortune. Have fun being creative and coming up with ways in which your bad luck is a necessary steppingstone to amazing good fortune. Let's imagine that you have just been to a job interview and it has been a total disaster. The fact that you are still in the job market means that you will now be motivated to apply for other jobs, and you might find an even better position than the one you were just interviewed for. Or perhaps you will go to a party, be offered a great life-changing opportunity, and now be in a position to take advantage of it.

Now ask yourself two questions—what evidence is there to suggest that these positive events won't actually happen? And what evidence is there to say that something even more positive won't come out of your ill fortune? The answer to both questions is "none." You have no idea what the future actually holds for you. All that is certain is that things will almost certainly be better if you don't let your bad luck get you down.

3. *Do not dwell on your ill fortune.*

Lucky people do not focus on the bad luck that has happened in the past but instead concentrate on the good fortune they have encountered and the great things that are going to happen in the future. If you experience bad luck, try not to dwell on your ill fortune; see what happens.

SUGGESTED EXERCISE

Distract Yourself

When they experienced bad luck, some lucky people said that they found it helpful spending about thirty minutes or so venting their negative emotions. Some cried, some took it out on a punching bag, and some went into an open field and screamed. But all lucky people agreed that it was really important not to dwell on their bad luck. Here are some tips for distracting your thoughts away from ill fortune:

- Go to the gym—exercise is a great way of taking your mind off your problems and also lifts your mood.

- Watch a funny film—choose a film that makes you laugh, and try your best to become involved in the story.

- Spend about twenty minutes thinking about a positive event that has happened to you in the past—something that made you feel really happy. If possible, look at some photographs taken at the time. Relive the event in your mind and think about how you felt at the time.

- Listen to music—again, choose something that makes you feel happy, and try your best to become involved in the music.

- Arrange to see your friends and talk about what's happening in their lives.

4. *Take constructive steps to prevent more bad luck in the future.*

Lucky people approach the problems in their lives in constructive ways. Instead of relying on superstition, they persist, learn from their past mistakes, and think through new and creative ways of tackling the bad luck that has happened. Do not be like unlucky Shelly, the woman who had several car crashes but didn't do anything to improve her driving skills because she blamed her misfortune on a series of jinxed cars. Instead, be like the lucky people who learn from the mistakes that they made in past job interviews and dates. When bad luck happens, do what lucky people do—take control of the situation and tackle the problem in a constructive way.

SUGGESTED EXERCISE

Take Five Steps to the Solution

Constructive problem solving involves five basic steps. Work your way through them when you encounter ill fortune and see what happens.

- First, don't assume that there is nothing you can do about the situation. Make a decision to take control and not be a victim of bad luck.

- Second, do something now. Not next week and not tomorrow, but right now.

- Third, make a list of all of your various options. Be creative. Think outside of the box. Try looking at the situation from different points of view. Brainstorm. Come up with as many potential solutions as possible, no matter how silly or absurd they may seem. Ask your friends what they

---

would do under the same circumstances. Keep on adding more and
more possible solutions.

- Fourth, decide on how you are going
to move forward. Consider each and
every possible solution. How long
will the solution take? Do you have
the knowledge and skills to implement
the solution? What are the likely
outcomes if you decide to adopt a
particular solution?

- Finally, and most important of all,
start to solve the problem. Obviously,
sometimes the solution might
involve waiting rather than rushing
to do something foolhardy—that's
fine, providing your inaction is part
of a plan and not simple procrastina-
tion. Also, be prepared to adapt your
solution as the future unfolds. Such
self-restraint and flexibility are key
aspects of being lucky. But the
important point is that you start to
concentrate on finding a solution
rather than fixating on the problem.

SUMMARY

The Four Principles And Twelve Subprinciples Of Luck

PRINCIPLE ONE: Maximize Your Chance Opportunities

Principle: Lucky people create, notice, and act upon the chance opportunities in their lives.

Subprinciples:
   1. Lucky people build and maintain a strong "network of luck."

2. Lucky people have a relaxed attitude toward life.

3. Lucky people are open to new experiences in their lives.

PRINCIPLE TWO: Listen to Your Lucky Hunches

Principle: Lucky people make successful decisions by using their intuition and gut feelings.

Subprinciples:
1. Lucky people listen to their gut feelings and hunches.

2. Lucky people take steps to boost their intuition.

PRINCIPLE THREE: Expect Good Fortune

Principle: Lucky people's expectations about the future help them fulfill their dreams and ambitions.

Subprinciples:
1. Lucky people expect their good luck to continue in the future.

2. Lucky people attempt to achieve their goals, even if their chances of success seem slim, and persevere in the face of failure.

3. Lucky people expect their interactions with others to be lucky and successful.

PRINCIPLE FOUR: Turn Your Bad Luck Into Good

Principle: Lucky people are able to transform their bad luck into good fortune.

Subprinciples:
1. Lucky people see the positive side of their bad luck.

2. Lucky people are convinced that any ill fortune in their lives will, in the long run, work out for the best.

3. Lucky people do not dwell on their ill fortune.

4. Lucky people take constructive steps to prevent more bad luck in the future.

SECTION THREE

Creating Luckier Lives

CHAPTER SEVEN

Luck School

My research has involved a large number of experiments, hundreds of interviews, and thousands of questionnaires. And throughout it I have managed to uncover the true secrets of luck. Luck is not a magical ability or a gift from the gods. Instead, it is a state of mind—a way of thinking and behaving. People are not born lucky or unlucky, but they create much of their own good and bad luck through their thoughts, feelings, and actions. The revelation is that a lucky life can be explained via four simple psychological principles. The first principle explains how lucky people's personalities help them create, notice, and act upon seemingly chance opportunities. Principle two reveals how lucky people's successful decisions revolve around a willingness to listen to their intuition and trust their lucky hunches. The third principle explains how lucky people's expectations about the future possess the power to become self-fulfilling prophecies and make their dreams come true. The fourth and final principle concerns how lucky people's resilient attitude and behavior can change bad luck into good.

The more I thought about my research, the more I became convinced that there was still one piece of the puzzle missing. Psychology is not just about understanding how people think, feel, and behave. Often, it is about change and transformation. It is about how to help people live happier and more satisfying lives. Could the four principles that I uncovered be used to increase the amount of good luck that people encounter in their lives? Would it be possible not only to explain luck, but also to create it?

People have searched for an effective way of improving the good fortune in their lives for many centuries.[1] Lucky charms, amulets, and talismans have been found in virtually all civilizations throughout recorded history. Touching wood dates back to pagan rituals that were designed to elicit the help of benign and powerful tree gods. The number thirteen is seen as unlucky because there were thirteen people at Christ's Last Supper. When a ladder is propped up against a wall it forms a natural triangle, which used to be seen as symbolic of the Holy Trinity. To walk under the ladder would break the Trinity and bring ill fortune.

Many of these beliefs and behaviors are still with us. In 1996, the Gallup Organization asked 1,000 Americans whether they were superstitious. Fifty-three percent said that they were at least a little superstitious, and twenty-five percent admitted to being somewhat or very superstitious.[2] Another survey revealed that seventy-two percent of the public said that they possessed at least one good-luck charm.[3] These high levels of superstitious thinking may represent only the tip of the iceberg, for research suggests that many people may be reluctant to admit to holding such beliefs. For example, several surveys have shown that only about twelve percent of people say that they avoid walking under ladders in the street. One British researcher wondered whether this really did reflect people's true level of superstitious belief and behavior. To find out, he positioned a ladder against a wall in a busy town center, and was amazed to discover that more than seventy percent of people risked stepping out into the street rather than walking under the ladder.[4]

Superstitious beliefs and behaviors have been passed down from generation to generation.

Our parents told us about them and we will pass them on to our children. But why do they persist? The answer lies in the power of luck. Throughout history, people have recognized that good and bad luck can transform lives. A few seconds of ill fortune can lay waste to years of striving, and moments of good luck can save an enormous amount of hard work. Superstition represents people's attempts to control and enhance this most elusive of factors. And the enduring nature of these superstitious beliefs and behaviors reflects the extent of people's desire to find ways of increasing their good luck. In short, superstitions were created, and have survived, because they promise that most elusive of holy grails—a way of enhancing good fortune.

There is just one problem. Superstition doesn't work. In the previous chapter I discussed how it was unlucky, rather than lucky, people who tended to engage in superstitious behavior. Several other researchers have also tested the validity of these age-old beliefs and found them wanting. My favorite experiment into the topic was a rather strange study conducted by high school student Mark Levin. In some countries, a black cat crossing your path is seen as lucky; in other countries it is seen as unlucky. Levin wanted to discover whether people's luck really changed when a black cat crossed their path. To find out, he asked

two people to try their luck at a simple coin tossing game. Next, a black cat was encouraged to
walk across their path, and the participants then
played the coin tossing game a second time. As a
control condi-
tion, Levin also
repeated the
experiment
using a white,
rather than a
black, cat. After
much coin
tossing and cat
crossing, Levin
concluded that
neither the
black nor white
cat had any
effect on par-
ticipants' luck.[5]

> "All of us have bad luck
> and good luck. The man
> who persists through the
> bad luck—who keeps right
> on going—is the man who
> is there when the good
> luck comes—and is ready
> to receive it."
>
> —ROBERT COLLIER

Superstition doesn't work because it is based
on out-of-date and incorrect thinking. It comes
from a time when people thought that luck was
a strange force that could only be controlled by
magical rituals and bizarre behaviors. My
research had revealed the real secrets that lie
behind a lucky life, and I wondered whether it
was possible to use this research to increase the
luck in people's lives. Would it be possible to

take people who were unlucky and make them lucky? Would it be possible to take lucky people and make them even luckier?

On New Year's Eve 1999 I was standing on the banks of the Thames in London. I was surrounded by thousands of people who were there to celebrate the new millennium. As midnight approached I wondered if it was now time to explore a far more scientific way of looking at a problem that has puzzled people for thousands of years. I wanted to see if it was possible to create new ways of helping people lead luckier lives. The type of techniques that I had in mind would not involve them crossing their fingers, touching wood, or avoiding ladders. Instead, people would be encouraged to incorporate the four principles of luck into their lives. It was time to encourage people to take the lucky charms out of their pockets and put them into their minds.

I decided to embark on a project to discover whether it is possible to enhance people's luck by getting them to think and behave like a lucky person. I wanted to send them to "Luck School" and discover if they could improve the fortune in their lives by following the principles and techniques you have read about.

The project consisted of two main parts. In the first part I met up with participants on a one-to-one basis and explained the rather unusual nature of the project. I also gave each of them a Luck Journal containing many of the questionnaires and exercises that you have already encountered in this book. I then asked them to complete three questionnaires. The first was the Luck Profile from page xix. This asked them to rate the degree to which they agree or disagree with statements relating to each of the subprinci-

> "Nobody gets justice. People only get good luck and bad luck."
> —ORSON WELLES

ples of luck. The second was the Luck Questionnaire from page 36. This presented them with descriptions of a typical lucky and unlucky person and asked them to rate the degree to which each of these descriptions applied to them. The third was the Life Satisfaction Questionnaire from page 42. This asked them to rate the degree to which they were satisfied with both their life as a whole and in five important sub-areas, namely, their family life, personal life, financial situation, health, and career. If you have been working your way through the exercises in this book, you will have already completed all three questionnaires. Both the Luck Questionnaire and the Life Satisfaction

Questionnaire gave me an accurate and objective measure of the participants' level of luck and life satisfaction prior to their incorporating the principles of luck into their life.

After they completed the questionnaires, I interviewed the participants about the role of luck in their lives. We chatted about many different topics, including whether they consider themselves lucky or unlucky, whether luck affects particular areas of their lives, whether they are outgoing, intuitive, and so on. I also asked them to complete versions of many of the exercises already described in this book, such as "Thinking about bad luck" (page 232) and "Attitudes toward ill fortune" (page 254).

Finally, I described the four main principles and twelve subprinciples of luck and explained how lucky people used these to create good fortune in their lives: how their personalities help them create, notice, and act upon seemingly chance opportunities (Principle One); how their successful decisions revolve around a willingness to listen to their intuition and trust their lucky hunches (Principle Two); how their expectations about the future become self-fulfilling prophecies that make their dreams come true (Principle Three); and how their resilient attitude toward ill fortune can transform bad luck into good (Principle Four). I briefly outlined the theories behind each of these principles and illustrated them with excerpts from my interviews with lucky and unlucky people and the results of my surveys and experiments. In short, I presented a summary of the information that you have already encountered in the previous chapters of this book.

In the second part of the project I met up with each participant, again on a one-to-one basis, about a week after our initial meeting. I explained the techniques that you have read about with each principle, and asked them to incorporate these techniques into their lives over the following month. This was, in many ways, the most important aspect of Luck School. To provide a clear picture of the way in which this part of the project was structured, we'll proceed in the next chapter as if you are one of the people participating.

CHAPTER EIGHT

Learning to Be Lucky

Welcome to Luck School. You have already read about the principles and subprinciples that lie behind a lucky life and have studied the practical techniques that will help you think and behave like a lucky person. In Luck School I would like you to incorporate these techniques into your life over the course of the following month and see if they make you luckier. In order to maximize the effectiveness of the course, I am going to lead you through five very different stages. Let's discuss each in turn.

Stage One: The Declaration

The first stage of the process involves you signing a special "luck declaration"—a simple statement of your intention to try to incorporate certain techniques into your life over the course of a month. This declaration springs from one simple question: Are you really prepared to invest a reasonable amount of time and effort into increasing your luck? If the answer is no, then there is little point in carrying on. I don't have a magic wand that I can simply wave to suddenly make you luckier. It doesn't work like that. If, however, you are prepared to at least try making some changes to the way in which you think and behave, then I would like you to copy the following sentence onto a new page in your Luck Journal:

> I want to increase the luck that I experience in my life, and am prepared to try to make the necessary changes in the way that I think and behave.

Now please sign your name under the declaration.

Thank you.

Stage Two:
Creating Your Luck Profile

You may remember that a little while ago you completed the Luck Profile (see page xix) and worked out your score on each of the four sections in the questionnaire (see Chapters Three, Four, Five, and Six). Look back at these four scores and then copy and complete the table on a new page in your Luck Journal. I have included a sample table here to illustrate how your final table should look.

Principle	Your Score	Low/Medium/High
1 Maximize your chance opportunities		
2 Listen to your lucky hunches		
3 Expect good fortune		
4 Turn bad luck into good		

Sample

Principle	Your Score	Low/Medium/ High
1 Maximize your chance opportunities	12	High
2 Listen to your lucky hunches	3	Low
3 Expect good fortune	11	Medium
4 Turn bad luck into good	18	High

This table represents a quick and easy way of seeing how you score on each of the four principles that underlie a lucky life. It also helps reveal the principles that you tend not to incorporate into your present-day thinking. When trying to change your luck, you can use this information to help you focus on the techniques that you need to incorporate into your life. So if, for example, you score low on Principle Two, then you need to think about how you might pay more attention to your intuition. If you obtain a medium score on Principle Three, then you might also benefit from focusing on how to increase your expectations of being luckier in the future. If you scored high on Principles One and Four, then there is probably less need to try to increase the chance opportunities in your life, or to improve your ability to turn bad luck into good.

Stage Three:
Incorporating the Techniques
Into Your Life

After each principle, I outlined techniques and exercises that will help you think and behave like a lucky person. Look at the ones that apply to the principle or principles that you need to enhance in your life. As you read through them again, think about how they could be applied in your everyday life over the course of the next four weeks.

So if, for example, you need to improve your intuition (Principle Two), you might want to enhance your ability to listen to your inner voice by carrying out exercises like "Visit the old man in the cave" (page 153) and "Make the decision, then stop" (page 155). You might also want to take some simple steps to boost your intuition, for instance by trying the exercise entitled "Make meditation matter" (page 156).

If, however, you need to increase the degree to which you expect good fortune in the future (Principle Three), you might want to review the exercises associated with each of the relevant subprinciples (such as "Affirm your luck" from page 220 and "Visualize good fortune" on page 227) and incorporate them into your life.

I have included a summary of the various exercises included throughout the book to help you identify the techniques and exercises that will have the greatest effect on your life.

Summary of Exercises

Principle One: Maximize your chance opportunities ...

1. **Build and maintain a strong "network of luck."**
   Connect four (page 101)
   Play the contact game (page 104)

2. **Develop a more relaxed attitude toward life.**
   Relax, then do it (page 106)

3. **Be open to new experiences in your life.**
   Play the dice game (page 109)

Principle Two: Listen to your lucky hunches ...

1. **Listen to your "inner voice."**
   Visit the old man in the cave (page 153)
   Make the decision, then stop (page 155)

2. **Take steps to boost your intuition.**
Make meditation matter (page 156)

Principle Three: Expect good fortune ...

1. **Expect good luck in the future.**
Affirm your luck (page 220)
Set lucky goals (page 221)

2. **Attempt to achieve your goals, even if your chances of success seem slim, and persevere in the face of failure.**
Carry out a cost-benefit analysis (page 224)

3. **Expect your interactions with others to be lucky and successful.**
Visualize good fortune (page 227)

Principle Four: Turn bad luck into good ...

1. **Look on the positive side of your bad luck.**
    Find the treasure in the trash (page 281)

2. **Remember that the ill fortune in your life may work out for the best.**
    Create a phoenix from the ashes (page 283)

3. **Do not dwell on your ill fortune.**
    Distract yourself (page 285)

4. **Take constructive steps to prevent more bad luck in the future.**
    Take five steps to the solution (page 287)

Stage Four:
Your Luck Journal

So far, we have talked through three of the stages involved in Luck School. In Stage One I asked you to write a brief declaration stating your intention to change. In Stage Two we reviewed your Luck Profile and identified which of the luck principles you could most benefit from. In Stage Three we talked through techniques for change and some exercises that will help you think and behave like a lucky person. Now we come to Stage Four. This is a vital part of the process and requires you to keep a diary of the lucky events that happen to you over the course of the next month.

Number the next thirty pages of your Luck Journal 1 to 30. At the end of each day, just spend a few moments writing down the lucky events that have happened to you. There is no need to write a long essay about each day; instead, just jot down a few words describing the good luck that you have encountered. Make a note of as many lucky events as possible. Remember to include events that seem relatively trivial as well as those that are more important.

Each morning, look back on the luck that you experienced the previous day.

Stage Five:
Final Thoughts

I always end each session with the following two thoughts.

First, take things one step at a time. Creating a lucky life will take a little time. Start off by connecting with a few more people, listening to your inner voice just a little more, having slightly higher expectations about the future, and so on. After a week or so you will probably encounter a small amount of additional good luck. This will then act as an important catalyst for further change. These small events will help you feel, think, and behave like a luckier person. And this, in turn, will cause you to incorporate the principles and techniques of luck into your life a little more. And so the process will continue. Slowly, but surely, you will become a luckier person.

Second, if I have learned anything over the last few years, it is that the good fortune experienced by lucky people is not the result of the gods smiling on them, or their being born lucky. Instead, without realizing it, lucky people have developed ways of thinking that make them especially happy, successful, and satisfied with their lives. In fact, these techniques are so effective that sometimes it appears as though lucky people are destined to lead charmed lives. But deep down, they are like everyone else. Deep down, they are just like you. And now that you know the techniques that they use, I believe that you can be just like them.

And all it will take is that little bit of effort that you promised in your declaration of luck.

CHAPTER NINE

Graduation Day

I met up with each participant who had taken part in Luck School about four weeks after asking them to change their thoughts and behavior, and had a long chat about what had happened. During this final interview, I asked them to review their Luck Journal and give an honest assessment as to whether the amount of luck that they encountered had increased, decreased, or remained the same. After the interview I also asked them to complete the Luck Questionnaire and the Life Satisfaction Questionnaire again.

I was able to analyze the results of the project in several different ways. First, in the final interview, everyone gave me an anecdotal account of the impact that the principles of luck had had on their lives. Second, I compared the ratings that they had given on the Luck Questionnaire and the Life Satisfaction Questionnaire in the first session with those given in the final session, to objectively measure whether they had become a luckier person and felt more satisfied with the various areas of their life.

This chapter outlines the results from Luck School. Some of the participants' names and earlier life experiences have already been mentioned in previous sections of the book; some of the cases that you are about to read are included for the first time.

Patricia's Story

Patricia, age twenty-eight, was one of the very first people to take part in Luck School. At our first meeting she explained that she has been unlucky for as long as she can remember.

A few years ago, she started to work as a flight attendant for a well-known airline and quickly gained a reputation among her colleagues as being something of a bad omen. On one of her first flights, a family became very drunk and abusive, and the flight had to make an unplanned landing in order for them to be off-loaded. A short while later, another of Patricia's flights was struck by lightning. Just weeks later, a third flight developed a fault with its braking system as it came in to land, resulting in the airplane being followed down the runway by fire engines.

Patricia's bad luck has also affected several other areas of her life. Like many unlucky people, Patricia is frequently delayed on transportation. She is convinced that she acts as a bad-luck charm and that her ill fortune can be transferred to those around her. Patricia now never wishes people good luck, because she thinks that in the past this has caused them to fail important interviews and exams. In my initial interview with Patricia, I asked her to explain how she felt when she experiences bad luck:

> I just think, "Oh, God, not again. Why can't something nice happen?" And wood is the bane of my life, because I'm forever touching it, just thinking, "Please let something nice happen." I am even unlucky when it comes to shopping. I'm just one of those people that if I see something that I like, then the shop doesn't have it in my size, or the one that I've chosen is ripped.

I also asked Patricia whether she thought that her bad luck would ever change. She was skeptical, and explained how she thought that some people are simply born unlucky and that there is very little they can do to change the situation.

Her Luck Profile and interview showed that she had low scores on all four principles of luck.

When I asked her about making friends and keeping in touch with people, she explained that she had relocated from another part of the country and so didn't know many people. She also described how she had grown apart from many of her friends and was very bad at keeping in touch with people.

Like many unlucky people, Patricia also said that she often didn't follow her intuition and then lived to regret it. Perhaps the most striking example of the negative impact that this had had on her life centered around her first serious relationship:

I think I was in the wrong place at the wrong time, and met a man that I really shouldn't have been with. I was with him for four and a half years. He was a control freak and it got to the point where I couldn't choose what to wear myself; he was choosing it for me. He had a reputation before I even started going out with him. My friends started telling me it was wrong two weeks into the relationship, and consistently told me for about two years and then gave up. I do have intuitive feelings, but I'm not sure if I

follow them. I don't think I trust myself
to trust my feelings.

Patricia also expected to be unlucky in the
future and did not cope well with ill fortune. I
asked her some of the questions that I had put
to many of the people involved in my research.
For example, I asked her about how she would
respond if she went on three dates, but they all
ended in failure. Patricia gave the type of reply
that was typical of an unlucky person:

> If I'd failed then I'd be a blubbering
> mess on the floor, thinking, "I'm a failure,
> help me." I always tend to find the bad
> side in whatever happens to me; it plays
> on my mind a lot. I'll be awake at night
> thinking about the bad side of things, or
> something that happened to me ten years
> ago thinking, "I wish I'd not said that."

At the end of the initial interview, I asked
Patricia to complete the Luck Questionnaire.
This presented her with a description of both a
typical lucky and unlucky person and asked her
to rate, on a scale between 1 ("doesn't describe
me at all") and 7 ("describes me very well"), the
degree to which each of these descriptions
applied to her. She gave a 2 to the description of

the typically lucky person, and a 6 to the description of the unlucky person. To obtain an overall luck score, I subtracted the rating that she had given to the unlucky description from the rating that she had given to the lucky description. Patricia had a luck score of -4 and so was classified as unlucky.

Patricia then completed the Life Satisfaction Questionnaire. This asked her to indicate the degree to which she was satisfied with her life as a whole, and with various sub-areas of her life such as her health, finances, family life, etc., by assigning a number between 1 (very dissatisfied) and 7 (very satisfied) to each area. Her scores, shown in the following graph, revealed that she was clearly dissatisfied with almost all aspects of her life.

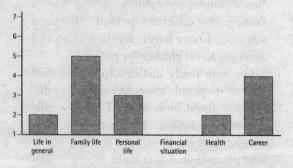

Patricia's scores on the Life Satisfaction Questionnaire

At our second session I explained some of my ideas about luck, and Patricia and I discussed how she might incorporate some simple luck techniques into her life. We talked about the importance of her listening to her inner voice (Principle Two: Subprinciple One), expecting good luck in the future (Principle Three: Subprinciple One), and avoiding dwelling on the bad fortune in her life (Principle Four: Subprinciple Three).

One month later, Patricia came back to see me again. She looked far more happy and relaxed, and cheerfully explained that her luck had undergone a dramatic transformation. For once, everything was working out her way:

> I'm impressed. I'm really impressed. I didn't think it would work, but it has. It has changed everything. I feel like a completely different person. It's been amazing, I have hardly any bad luck at all now. It's a real change for me.
>
> Our talk really instilled in me the fact that some people thought completely differently about luck, which I hadn't really considered before. I didn't think that people thought they were really lucky; I was amazed that that went through people's minds. So opening my eyes to that

made me think, 'Well, there's no reason why I can't do this." And as time was going on, more and more good things were happening and less and less bad things. It started to have a real effect then. It was just small things at first, but that made me feel more positive about life, and it started to seep in.

In the first week, I went out to buy a coat that I'd seen a few weeks before. I used to be so unlucky shopping, I used to dread it. I thought that the chances of it still being there were slim, but decided to make myself go for it. So I went into the store, and the coat was still there. The store only had one left, but it was my size, and I bought it. That's never happened before, it's unprecedented. And I used to always miss the bus. But that week the bus was there when I arrived. It hadn't driven off, and I managed to get it. I didn't use to get it at all, not even once a week. Now I catch it all the time. It's amazing.

After the first week, I thought, "I wonder if it's going to be a short-term thing?" but what really surprised me was that it continued. It was just something that was happening. After a while I didn't even have to think about it anymore. It's made a significant difference to my life.

Like the other day, my parents bought me a surprise computer. But there was something missing from it. Normally I would just give up and leave it, but instead I decided to turn my bad luck into good. I decided to go into town and get the missing part. I went out in my car on a busy Saturday afternoon and instantly found a parking space. When I got to the store, I found that I hadn't brought any money with me. I turned around, and there was a cash machine, and it was working. And then, as I got to the store, it was just about to close. But I had a quick chat with the sales assistant and she let me in, and I managed to get the missing part—in fact, it was the last one that they had in stock. These sorts of things have never happened to me before—it's amazing—I was very surprised. I was amazed and had to tell everyone.

Patricia had managed to incorporate Principles Two and Three into her life. She described the major role that listening to her intuition and having lucky expectations about the future had played in her transformation:

I have tried being more intuitive. To take some time out and listen to my inner voice. The day after I went to the computer shop, something flashed in my mind. I just knew that I should save the work that I had written on my computer. So I did, and then the computer suddenly crashed! But my work was saved, so that was really positive.

And being positive about the future has helped, too. When I first started off, I had to force myself to start the day thinking about the affirmations— "today's going to be a really lucky day" and all that. But after a while I didn't have to do that anymore, because it was more subconscious and automatic. As time was going on I was becoming more accustomed to it. Both my boyfriend and parents have definitely noticed a change. I now feel far more positive about the future, which is amazing, because to make me positive is a real achievement. It's definitely had an amazing effect. I don't think of myself as being particularly unlucky anymore.

Also, Patricia had found that not dwelling on her bad luck, taking control, and looking on the positive side of the negative events that happened to her had softened the emotional impact of bad luck and helped her adopt a far more constructive approach to the ill fortune she encountered.

I've managed to turn around some of the unlucky things that have happened. I've stopped being so superstitious and not knocked wood so much.

Unlucky things still happen—my car has broken down, and my television has just stopped working, but I don't seem to notice these sorts of little things anymore. They're definitely not dwelling on my mind as much. It's definitely made a difference, because bad luck doesn't drag me down now. In the past I'd miss the bus, and then something else would happen, and then there would be a pile of unlucky events, and I'd get really fed up. But now if I miss the bus I can think through how it's not really an issue, how it doesn't really matter compared to the important things in my life. I just don't even think about it. And it's made me feel a lot more in control. I think I'm a bit more of a master of what happens to me rather than waiting for events to happen to me.

When my car broke down, before taking part in this, the first thing on my mind would have been, "It always happens to me, it never happens to anybody else." And now it's, "All right, well how am I going to deal with it now?" So it's more positive and constructive. I just think, "Right, what are the actions I'm going to have to take now? I need to get it sorted out so let's not dwell on it. There's no point, it won't get you anywhere, just get on with it."

And a few weeks ago I needed a dress for a dance that I was going to. I went shopping, and found a dress that I really liked, but I didn't buy it, because I thought, "I will go back in a week and if it's still there, then it's passed the luck test and I'll buy it." So I went back and it wasn't there! In the past I'd have just stormed out of the store, become depressed, been really miserable, and probably not have gone to the dance. But instead, I looked on the bright side and thought, "Well, maybe there's something else," so I went and looked, and I found something else that was better, and it was cheaper, and it looked fantastic. So I was so happy and went to the dance feeling really good.

At the end of Luck School, I asked Patricia to think back to her level of luck before the study and assess the degree to which it had changed. Patricia said that her luck had increased by 75 percent. Finally, I asked her to complete the Luck Questionnaire and the Life Satisfaction Questionnaire one last time. Before taking part in the project, her Luck Score was −4. Afterward, it had risen to +3. Patricia had transformed from an unlucky to a lucky person. Perhaps most important of all, her scores on the final Life Satisfaction Questionnaire revealed that she was now highly satisfied with all areas of her life.

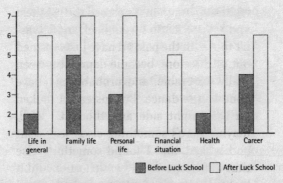

Patricia's scores on the Life Satisfaction Questionnaire

Carolyn's Story

During her first week at Luck School, Carolyn described how she had been consistently unlucky throughout her life:

One time, loads of really unlucky things happened in just three days. I was playing with my thirteen-year-old daughter. I fell down a foot hole that I knew was there anyway, and hit my head against a wall. Not thinking I'd done too much damage, we drove 200 miles home. That evening I collapsed, hit my head again, and gave myself a concussion. I went to my doctor and was given medication. But to take the medication I had to eat three times a day. The next day I cracked my tooth on a bag of chips, but I couldn't have my tooth fixed because I was on the medication. And then I backed my car into a tree, causing a large amount of damage. The following day I couldn't move—it turned out that I had damaged the base of my back, but the medication for the concussion had dampened the pain so I hadn't noticed it. I spent three weeks resting in bed. And this is the way my whole life goes.

I am so unlucky when it comes to financial matters. My aunt had breast cancer and I'd been her caregiver for four years. We were very close, and I asked if she would agree to me buying her house from her. We both thought that it was a good idea. I set up a huge bank loan and mortgage to pay off the property. The day the forms came through she didn't look very well. So I took her to the doctor's, and she'd had a suspected stroke and wasn't well enough to go to the lawyers to sign the forms. Two weeks later I booked another appointment with the lawyers and that morning she had a massive stroke and never fully recovered. So now I've lost my aunt, the house, and have a real financial mess to sort out.

At the end of her first interview, I asked Carolyn to complete the Luck Questionnaire and the Life Satisfaction Questionnaire. She obtained a luck score of –3 and was clearly dissatisfied with almost all areas of her life.

Carolyn and I discussed ways in which she could incorporate all four luck principles into her life. When Carolyn returned a month later, she was a different person.

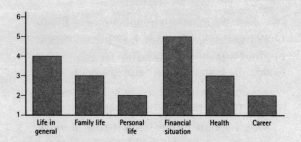

*Carolyn's scores on the Life Satisfaction Questionnaire
before Luck School*

I have been surprised by it all. When I started I wasn't certain what was going to happen. And then, just a few weeks later, everything has changed. I am far luckier. And my friends have really noticed a difference. I've been smiling a lot more. I go out far more positive, I don't go out thinking I'm going to be unlucky. It's even rubbed off on my best friend. Now he doesn't even go out thinking that I am going to be a loser. I am really pleased because things have changed. As I look back, it all feels very strange.

Carolyn had found it very helpful to use various techniques to look on the positive side of her ill fortune (Principle Four: Subprinciple One) and also to take a more constructive approach to the bad luck that she encountered (Principle Four: Subprinciple Four):

Many aspects of my life have improved. I have passed my driving test after three years of trying, won money in competitions, and am much happier. One major change is that I think through how I can solve problems in my life rather than put them down to bad luck My house is falling apart, so I called my local housing board. The woman there didn't call me back, so I called her back again, she still wouldn't talk to me because she was too busy. So, rather than letting it go, I decided to persist. I thought about what a huge change it could make to my life and that it would only involve a phone call or two. So I kept on going. I called up the head office and I asked to speak to someone in charge. They put me through to the director's personal assistant, and I spoke to her and explained all my gripes. She called up my housing official that day and complained to her for me. A few days ago, the two of them came out and agreed to do all the work on my property. They've completed all the gardening work in the last week and they're going to complete all the building renovations that needed to be done—I've waited three years for this. And it's because of me thinking that I was really lucky instead of assuming that nothing will change.

At the end of the interview, Carolyn said that her luck had improved by 85 percent. Her ratings on the final Luck Questionnaire showed that her luck score had increased from –3 to an amazing +6, and her ratings on the final Life Satisfaction Questionnaire also showed a huge improvement across all areas of her life.

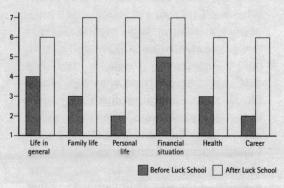

Carolyn's scores on the Life Satisfaction Questionnaire

Other Graduates

Patricia and Carolyn were typical of many other unlucky people who enrolled in Luck School. In Chapter Four I described the unlucky life of Marilyn. She had remained in two disastrous relationships despite her inner voice telling her to leave. She kindly agreed to take part in Luck School. After a few weeks, Marilyn was far more upbeat and said that her luck had improved by 40 percent. Much of this improvement revolved around her ability to increase the number of chance opportunities in her life (Principle One) and develop lucky expectations about the future (Principle Three):

I decided to take control of my life and introduce some variety into it. I started a new job as an advertising consultant for a magazine, and I love it. I've also started doing Tupperware parties as well. I'm doing my first one next weekend. I also filled out an application form for one of those "reality TV shows." They asked me to make a short video and send it to them. So I imagined myself being lucky and thought about the type of video that would appeal to them. In the end, I climbed into a huge box, had someone wrap it up with a big bow, and then videotaped myself popping out and shouting, "Surprise, you've got the winning video, you're looking at the first member of the team." It was a few minutes long, just me telling them a bit about myself and why I wanted to be on the show. If I get an interview I'll be happy. I reckon I'd be very good on it. I applied last year, but I was feeling really unlucky, and my video was awful. My application form was awful, too. I just didn't come across very well. Things are also going really well on the boyfriend front. For the first time I sat down and thought very carefully about what my intuition was telling me. I realized that I felt very positively toward him. It felt perfect! Absolutely perfect. We are going to Paris soon. He threw me a surprise party for my birthday. It's fantastic. I am really, really happy in the relationship, 10 out of 10.

I was keen to discover whether it would be possible to make lucky people even luckier, and so was delighted whenever lucky people agreed to take part in the project.

In Chapters Three and Six I described the lucky life of Joseph, the thirty-five-year-old student. When he was younger, Joseph was in constant trouble with the police. Then, a chance conversation with a psychology teacher on a train changed his life. The teacher was impressed with Joseph's insight into his behavior and suggested that he would make an excellent psychologist. Joseph decided to take control, looked into the type of qualifications required, and eventually decided to return to college. Joseph also has the ability to turn bad luck into good. In Chapter Six, I described how he softens the emotional impact of any bad luck in his life by taking the long view, and noted how he described being sent to prison as one of the luckiest things that ever happened to him. When he agreed to take part in Luck School, Joseph was studying for a degree in psychology and hoped to graduate and find work as a counselor.

When we first met to discuss the project, I asked Joseph to complete a Luck Questionnaire and Life Satisfaction Questionnaire. Perhaps not surprisingly, Joseph had a luck score of +5, and was very satisfied with many areas of his life. But would it be possible to make him even luckier?

When I reviewed the techniques that lucky people used to create good fortune in their lives, Joseph quickly realized that he was already using many of these techniques but agreed to make a conscious effort to apply them more often over the coming weeks. In particular, he thought that he might benefit from reducing the impact of bad luck (Principle Four; Subprinciples One, Two, Three, and Four). We also discussed how he might increase the number of chance opportunities he encountered in his life (Principle One: Subprinciples One, Two, and Three).

One month later I met with Joseph again and he told me what had happened. He started off

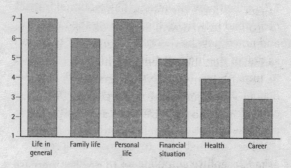

Joseph's scores on the Life Satisfaction Questionnaire before

Luck School

by describing how he had managed to increase his ability to look on the positive side of ill fortune (Principle Four: Subprinciple One):

A couple of unlucky things happened, and they would have brought me down if

I hadn't been able to see how some good luck might come out of them. I was a bit like that before, but even more so now.

The other day I went home, and my wife told me that I have to talk to my son because he was caught stealing some food from the cafeteria at his school. It's the first time he's ever done anything like this and fortunately he got caught, so now I can reinforce the message that this isn't an avenue to go down. So a bit of bad luck in his case has turned into good luck. It's lucky that he's been caught for it now, because in my case years ago, when I was a mischievous boy, I never got caught the first time, so because I got away with it I thought I was invincible, and carried on.

Joseph had also managed to greatly increase the number of chance opportunities in his life (Principle One: Subprinciples One, Two, and Three):

Lots of my good luck over the past few weeks has centered around opportunities. Just small things at first, but they really built up. The other day, I walked past another student. I don't know him very well, but I thought I'd stop and talk. I said hello and he asked me how things were going. I told him that I was taking a statistics course, but that my statistics aren't that great, and my lecturer had recommended this book, but when I went down to the bookshop I found out it was really expensive. Anyway, this guy said that he had the book and gave it to me for free, because he had already finished the course.

A few weeks ago I was walking back to my car in the garage and I saw a piece of paper on the ground. Normally I would have walked past it, but instead I treated it as an opportunity! I kicked it, just in case it was a lottery ticket, or something like that. Anyway, I kicked at the paper, and there was a $20 bill underneath. And when I picked it up I realized it was five $20 bills—$100 in cash. It was just lying there.

But the big news is that I was headhunted. I work voluntarily for an organization that helps people who have learning disabilities integrate into the community. Another charity heard about me and they sent me a letter saying they understand the work I'm doing and offered me a job to go out to people who feel they can live in the community but who have learning difficulties. My job would be to go and assess if that is the case. Initially for the first year they said they can offer me part-time, paid, work. It's perfect because it works in with my university classes because it's only three hours a day four days a week. This is the type of work I want to get into, this is what I've always wanted.

The whole thing has been wonderful, much better than I expected. I've had an excellent time. I always had a lucky outlook, but it is especially positive now. Other people have noticed some kind of change. They have become more positive with me.

Joseph said that his luck had increased by 50 percent. His luck score had increased from +5

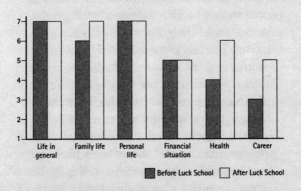

Joseph's scores on the Life Satisfaction Questionnaire

to +6, and his scores on the final Life Satisfaction Questionnaire showed that he was now even more satisfied with his life.

Summing Up

In total, 80 percent of people who attended Luck School said that their luck had increased. On average, these people estimated that their luck had increased by more than 40 percent. After Luck School, people's luck scores revealed that unlucky people had become lucky, and lucky people had become even luckier. Perhaps most important of all, as shown in the following graph, the participants had become far more satisfied with all aspects of their lives.[1]

My previous research into luck predicted that people should be able to increase the good fortune in their lives by simply thinking and behaving like lucky people. Luck School has demonstrated that this prediction is correct. Unlucky people have become lucky, and lucky people have become even luckier. Even over the course of just a month, the effects have been dramatic. People have created more chance opportunities, made more lucky decisions, taken important steps toward realizing their lifelong ambitions, and developed ways of transforming their bad luck into good.

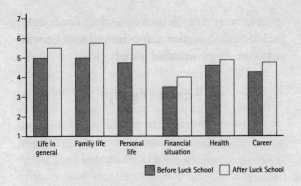

Average scores on the Life Satisfaction Questionnaire

Toward a Luckier Future

At the very start of the book I described how my background as a professional magician led me to become interested in academic psychology. When I was a magician I needed to understand how my audience perceived the world in order to create magic tricks that fooled and entertained them. Now that I have reached the end of my investigations into luck, I realize that there exists a far deeper connection between my previous work as a magician and my present-day research. As a magician, I appeared to make the impossible possible. Objects vanished into thin air and defied the laws of gravity.

People were sawed in half and then emerged unharmed. For just a few minutes, the world was transformed into a very different place. Likewise, my research into luck illustrates the potential for transformation. It demonstrates how people can dramatically increase the luck in their lives. It shows how they can change and grow, and how they can leave the past behind and move toward a luckier and more satisfying future.

But unlike the tricks that I performed as a magician, this transformation is not a fleeting illusion created by clever sleight of hand. Instead, it is a permanent and genuine change based upon four powerful psychological principles. And it doesn't involve any arcane knowledge or years of dedicated practice. Instead, it simply requires a firm understanding of the ideas described in this book and a genuine desire to incorporate the four luck principles and lead a luckier life.

Discovering the hidden secrets of luck has been a long but rewarding journey. For thousands of years people have recognized the importance of luck but assumed that it was a mystical force that could only be influenced by superstitious rituals. They have tried to increase the luck in their lives by carrying lucky charms, touching wood, and avoiding the

number thirteen. None of these techniques
have worked because such superstitious thinking is based on an incorrect understanding of
luck. Scientific research has revealed that the
real explanation of luck lies in four basic psychological principles. This book has both
explained the theory behind these four principles and described the practical techniques to
help you incorporate them into your life. These
techniques have the potential to enhance the
good fortune that you encounter on a daily
basis and enrich your life. They can make
unlucky people lucky, and lucky people even
luckier.

Of course, whether you decide to use these
techniques is up to you. Only you can decide
whether you want to change the way you think
and behave. But before you make that decision,
consider the effects that some additional good
luck could have on both your personal and professional life. Think of how harnessing good
fortune could help create a happy family life
and a close circle of loyal friends; how it could
help you find your dream job and perfect partner; and how it could help you live a healthy,
happy, and highly satisfied life. Making the
necessary changes will not be difficult or time-
consuming. All you need is a genuine desire for
transformation and a willingness to view your

luck in a radically new way. Your future isn't set in stone. You are not destined to always experience a certain amount of good fortune. You can change. You can create far more lucky breaks and greatly increase how often you are in the right place at the right time.

When it comes to luck, the future is in your hands.

And it starts right now.

Appendices

APPENDIX A

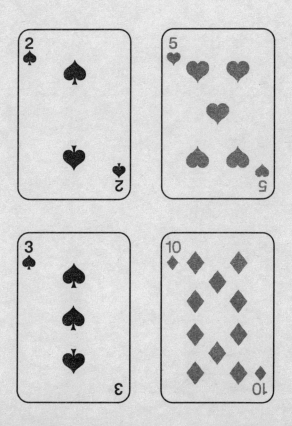

APPENDIX B

Analyst 1

Analyst 2

Notes

INTRODUCTION

1.   See, e.g., Wiseman, R. 1997. *Deception and Self-Deception: Investigating Psychics*. Buffalo, NY: Prometheus Press.

2.   See, e.g., Wiseman, R. 1995. The MegaLab truth test. *Nature* 373: 391; Lamont, P. and Wiseman, R. 1997. *Magic in Theory: An Introduction to the Theoretical and Psychological Elements in Conjuring*. Seattle: Hermetic Press.

CHAPTER ONE

1.   Bechtel, S. and Stains, L. R. 1997. *The Good Luck Book*. New York: Workman Publishing, p. 195.

2.   *The Fortean Times*, December 2001. Issue 153, p. 6.

3.   Simmons, I. 1996. *The Fortean Times Book of Life's Losers*. London: John Brown Publishing, p. 60.

4.   *The Good Luck Book*, op. cit., p. 203.

5.   Bandura, A. 1982. The psychology of chance encounters and life paths. *American Psychologist* 37(7): 747–755.

6.   See, for example:

       Williams, E. N., Soeprapto, E., Like, K., Touradji, P., Hess, S. and Hill, C. E. 1998. Perceptions of serendipity: Career paths of prominent academic women in counseling psychology. *Journal of Counseling Psychology* 45: 379–389.

       Krumboltz, J. D. 1998. Serendipity is not serendipitous. *Journal of Counseling Psychology*, 45(4): 390–392.

       Mitchell, K. E., Levin, A. S. & Krumboltz, J. D. 1999. Planned happenstance: Constructing unexpected career opportunities. *Journal of Counseling and Development* 77(2): 115–124.

7.   From Krumboltz, op. cit. p. 391.

8.   Brian, D. 2001. *Pulitzer: A Life*. New York: John Wiley & Sons.

9.   Wreden, N. 2002. How to make your case in 30 seconds or less. *Harvard Management Communication Letter*, p. 3.

10.   MacLaine, S. 1970. *Don't Fall Off the Mountain*. New York: W. W. Norton.

11.   *The Good Luck Book*, op., cit. p. 141.

12.   *Today*, 13 October 1995, p. 7.

13.   Roberts, R. M. 1989. *Serendipity*. New York: John Wiley & Sons.

14.   *The Good Luck Book*, op. cit., p. 176.

15.   Additional information about the type of questions used in this survey can be found in:

      Wiseman, R., Harris, P. & Middleton, W. 1994. Luckiness and psi: An initial survey. *Journal of the Society for Psychical Research* 60(836): 115. This paper also describes an experiment that hinted at a possible relationship between luck and psychic ability. Unfortunately, this finding was not replicated in subsequent research.

CHAPTER TWO

1. See, for example:

   Greene, F. M. 1960. The feeling of luck and its effect on PK. *Journal of Parapsychology* 24: 129-141.

   Ratte, R. 1960. Comparison of game and standard PK testing techniques under competitive and non-competitive conditions. *Journal of Parapsychology* 24(4): 235–244.

   For a review of work examining the relationship between luck and psychic ability see:

   Smith, M. D., Wiseman, R., Harris, P., and Joiner, R. 1996. On being lucky: The psychology and parapsychology of luck. *European Journal of Parapsychology* 12: 35–43.

2. This work was carried out in collaboration with Dr. Matthew Smith and Dr. Peter Harris.

3. The experiment involved 728 participants (245 lucky people, 295 neutral people, and 188 unlucky people). Everyone returned a questionnaire stating how many tickets they intended to buy for the forthcoming lottery draw and the numbers that they intended to select. After the draw had taken place, we calculated their overall level of profit or loss, and how many numbers they had correctly matched, averaged across the number of tickets that they had bought. Two unpaired T-tests revealed that the lucky and unlucky groups did not differ on either measure (Profit/loss: df = 431, T-value [unpaired] = .41: P-value [2-tailed] = .68: Average numbers matched; df = 431, T-value [unpaired] = .24, P-value [2-tailed] = .81).

4. For an up-to-date and very readable review of previous research concerning measures of life satisfaction, see:

    Argyle, M. 2001. *The Psychology of Happiness*. London: Routledge.

5. This study involved 50 lucky people, 115 neutral people, and 35 unlucky people. Six Kruskal-Wallis tests were carried out to compare the scores of the three groups

on each of the items within the Life Satisfaction Questionnaire. The resulting H-values and associated P-values are shown in the following table:

	H-value corrected for ties)	P-value (2-tailed)
Life in general	38.72	.0001
Family life	8.78	.01
Personal	9.25	.01
Financial situation	21.56	.0001
Health	13.48	.001
Career	21.96	.0001

6.   For additional details see:

Wiseman, R. & Watt, C. 2002. Belief in the paranormal, cognitive ability and extrasensory perception: The role of experimenter effects. *Proceedings of the 45th Annual Convention of the Parapsychological Association. Paris, France.*

7.   Participants were asked "How confident are you of winning something in the lottery this week?" and indicated their

answers on a scale between 1 (Not at all confident) and 7 (Extremely confident). The Kruskal-Wallis analysis comparing the scores of the three groups was highly significant (df = 2, H-value [corrected for ties] = 216.70, P-value [2-tailed] < .0001).

CHAPTER THREE

1. For an excellent introduction to personality research, see:

    Furnham, A. & Heaven, P. 1999. *Personality and Social Behaviour*. London: Arnold.

2. The NEO FFI was administered to 19 lucky and 14 unlucky people. Unpaired T-tests revealed that their scores did not differ on either agreeableness (df = 31, T-value [unpaired] = -.11, P-value [2-tailed] =.91) or conscientiousness (df = 31, T-value [unpaired] = 1.06, P-value [2-tailed] = .30).

3. An unpaired T-test revealed that lucky people had significantly higher extroversion scores than unlucky people (df = 31, T-value [unpaired] = 4.11, P-value [2-tailed] = .0003).

4. For an accessible introduction to psychological research into nonverbal communication, see relevant sections in:

Argyle, M. 1988. *Bodily Communication*. London: Routledge.

5. An unpaired T-test revealed that unlucky people had significantly higher neuroticism scores than lucky people (df = 31, T-value [unpaired] = 5.16, P-value [2-tailed] < .0001).

6. An unpaired T-test revealed that lucky people had significantly higher openness scores than unlucky people (df = 31, T-value [unpaired] = 2.09, P-value [2-tailed] = .04).

CHAPTER FOUR

1. See Bennett, O. 1997. The best of luck. *The Independent on Sunday*, 23 March, p. 6.

2. For a good overview of this work, see:

Claxton, G. 1998. *Hare Brain Tortoise Mind*. London: Fourth Estate.

3.   Kunst-Wilson, W. R., & Zajoc, R. B. 1980. Affective discrimination of stimuli that cannot be recognized. *Science*, 207, 557–558.

4.   Bornstein, R. F. 1989. Exposure and affect: Overview and meta-analysis of research, 1968–1987. *Psychological Bulletin*, 106: 265-289.

5.   Hill presented students with several pictures of faces. These had been manipulated to ensure that the distance between the eyes and chin was either relatively small or relatively large. When the distance was small, the face looked short, and when the distance was large, the face looked long. Everyone was told that these were faces of university professors and that these professors varied in how fair they were as teachers. Half the participants were told that the two professors with long faces were fair and that the two people with short faces were unfair. These descriptions were reversed for the other half of the participants. They were told that the two professors with long faces were unfair and the two people with short faces were fair.

Everyone was then given some additional faces and asked to rate them for fairness. One of the faces was long and the other was short. The results were startling. The participants who had been shown long faces and told that they were fair, rated the long-faced person as much fairer than the short-faced person. In contrast, the participants who had been shown long faces and told that they were unfair, rated the long-faced person as less fair than the short-faced person. When asked to explain why they had assigned their ratings to the faces, none mentioned being influenced by the initial faces. Instead, they said it felt as if they had just followed their intuition. But without knowing it, the participants had subconsciously detected a pattern in the initial faces and applied it to the new faces. Without realizing it, their subconscience had caused them to instantly have a gut feeling about these new people and see them in a certain way.

For further information, see:

Hill, T., Lewicki, P., Czyzewska, M., and Schuller, G. 1990. The role of learned inferential encoding rules in the per-

ception of faces: Effects of noncon-
scious self-perpetuation of a bias.
*Journal of Experimental Social
Psychology* 26(4): 350–371.

6.   I have also carried out this experiment
showing the long-faced analysts as unsuccessful and the short-faced ones as successful—under these conditions, the
number of people choosing Analyst 1
drops from 90 percent to just 50 percent.

CHAPTER FIVE

1.   One hundred and sixty-six people partici-
pated in this study (39 lucky people, 99
neutral people, and 28 unlucky people).
Everyone was asked to assess the likelihood of experiencing the listed event in
the future by assigning the event a number between 0 (will never happen) and
100 (certain to happen). The results of the
Kruskal-Wallis analyses comparing the
groups are shown in the following table.
Initial data for this study was collected in
collaboration with Dr. Matthew Smith
and Dr. Peter Harris.

	H-value (corrected for ties)	P-value (2-tailed)
Being admired for your accomplishments	17.02	.0002
Having an out-of-town friend visit you	7.01	.03
Developing or maintaining a good relationship with your family	7.68	.021
Achieving at least one of your life's ambitions	13.52	.001
Being given $250 just to spend on yourself	14.26	.0008
Having a great time on your next vacation	28.74	.0001
Looking young for your age when you are older	4.56	.10
Having someone tell you that you are talented	15.08	.0005
Average score	23.41	.0001

2. The results of the Kruskal-Wallis analyses

comparing the groups are shown in the following table.

	H-value (corrected for ties)	P-value (2-tailed)
Being the victim of a mugging	1.92	.38
Attempting suicide	7.32	.03
Suffering severe depression	11.08	.004
Having an alcohol problem	2.27	.32
Deciding you chose the wrong career	1.54	.46
Having insomnia every night of the week	9.90	.007
Becoming seriously overweight later in life	7.32	.03
Contracting meningitis	.26	.88
Average score	8.17	.02

3.   Rosenthal, R. and Jacobson, L. F. 1968.

Pygmalion in the Classroom. New York: Holt, Rinehart, & Winston.

4. For a review of this work, see:

Snyder, M. 1984. When belief creates reality. In L. Berkowitz (ed.), *Advances in Experimental Social Psychology* (vol. 18, pp. 248–306). New York: Academic Press.

5. For a review of this work, see:

Scheier, M. and Carver, C. 1987. Dispositional optimism and physical well-being: The influence of generalised outcome expectations on health. *Journal of Personality* 55: 169–210.

Kavussanu, M. and McAuley, E. 1995. Exercise and optimism: Are highly active individuals more optimistic? *Journal of Sport and Exercise Psychology* 39: 1031–9.

Taylor, S. T. and Armor, D. A. 1996. Positive illusions and coping with adversity. *Journal of Personality* 64(4): 873–898.

6. Everson, S., Goldberg, D., Kaplan, G., et al. 1996. Hopelessness and risk of mortality and

incidence of myocardial infarction and cancer. *Psychosomatic Medicine*, 58: 113–121.

7.   See, for example:

Hansen, C. 1989. A causal model of the relationship among accidents, biodata, personality and cognitive factors. *Journal of Applied Psychology* 74: 81–90.

8.   Phillips, D. P., Liu, G. C., Kwok, K., Jarvinen, J. R., Zhang, W. and Abramson, I. S. 2001. *The Hound of the Baskervilles* effect: natural experiment on the influence of psychological stress on timing of death. *British Medical Journal* 323: 1443–1446.

9.   Dougherty, T. W., Turban, D. B. and Callender, J. C. 1994. Confirming first impressions in the employment interview: A field study of interviewer behavior. *Journal of Applied Psychology* 79(5): 659–665.

10.   Livingston, J. S. 1988. Pygmalion in management. *Harvard Business Review* (September-October): 121–130.

11.   Snyder, M., Tanke, E. D. and Berscheid, E. 1977. Social perception and interpersonal

behaviour: On the self-fulfilling nature of social stereotypes. *Journal of Personality and Social Psychology* 35: 656–666.

CHAPTER SIX

1. Medvec, V. H., Madey, S. F., and Gilovich, T. 1995. When less is more: Counterfactual thinking and satisfaction among Olympic medallists. *Journal of Personality and Social Psychology* 69: 4, 603–610.

2. For an additional discussion on the relationship between counterfactual thinking and luck, see:

   Teigen, K. H. 1995. How good is good luck? The role of counterfactual thinking in the perception of lucky and unlucky events. *European Journal of Social Psychology* 25: 281–302.

3. Laird, J. D., Wagener, J. J., Halal, M. and Szegda, M., 1982. Remembering what you feel: effects of emotion on memory. *Journal of Personality and Social Psychology* 42(4): 646–657.

4. This study involved 28 participants (17 lucky and 11 unlucky). Everyone was asked

to complete a questionnaire that contained three items concerning well-known superstitions about black cats, breaking a mirror, and the number thirteen. Participants rated each statement on a scale between 1 (disagree) and 7 (agree). Their responses to the items were summed to create a single score, and revealed significant differences between the groups.

CHAPTER SEVEN

1. The ancient roots of many superstitions are presented in Gwathmey, E. 1994. *Lots of Luck: Legend and Lore of Good Fortune.* California: Angel City Press.

2. Moore, D. W. 2000. One in four Americans superstitious. Gallup Poll News Service. October 13.

3. Epstein, S. 1993. Cognitive-experiential self theory: Implications for developmental psychology. In M. Gunnar and L. A. Sroufe (eds.), Self-processes and development. *Minnesota Symposia on Child Psychology,* (vol 23, pp. 79–123), Hillsdale, NJ: Erlbaum.

4. Garwood, K. 1963. Superstition and half belief. *New Society* (31 January): 13–14.

5. Levin, M. Do black cats cause bad luck? Winner of the Joel Serebin Memorial Essay Contest organized by the New York Area Skeptics. http://www.webmonkey-dean.com/dean/quotes.blackcats.

CHAPTER NINE

1. Participants were asked to complete the Luck Questionnaire and the Life Satisfaction Questionnaire both prior to, and after attending, Luck School. Two Wilcoxon signed-rank tests were used to compare their luck score and average score on the Life Satisfaction Questionnaire pre- and post-study. Both were significant (luck score: Z [corrected for ties] = -2.51, P-value [2-tailed] = .01: mean score on the Life Satisfaction Scale: Z [corrected for ties] = -2.04, P-value [2-tailed] = .04).

Order These Great True Crime Books:

Please send the books checked below:

	Price Ea.	Qty.	Total
☐ **Sex, Power & Murder** — Chandra Levy and Gary Condit: the affair that shocked America	$5.99		
☐ **They're Killing Our Children** — Inside the kidnapping and child murder epidemic sweeping America	$6.99		
☐ **JonBenet** — The police files	$7.99		
☐ **Sixteen Minutes From Home** — The Columbia Space Shuttle tragedy	$5.99		
☐ **Saddam** — The face of evil	$5.99		
☐ **The Murder of Laci Peterson**	$5.99		
☐ **Diana** — Secrets & Lies	$5.99		
☐ **Martha Stewart** — Just Desserts	$6.99		
☐ **Driven to Kill** — The Clara Harris story	$5.99		
Postage & Handling: U.S., $ 2.75 for one book, $ 1.00 for each additional			
Total enclosed:			

Ship to:

NAME _____

ADDRESS _____

CITY _____ STATE _____ ZIP _____

Order These Great Celebrity Books:

Please send the books checked below:

Order These Great Health & Fitness Books:

Please send the books checked below:

	Price Ea.	Qty.	Total
☐ *Instant Weight Loss* — Lose 10 pounds in 10 days — and keep it off!	$5.99		
☐ *No More Diets ... Ever* — The breakthrough plan that will change your life	$5.99		
☐ *The Ultimate Low-Carb Plan* — The last diet book you'll ever buy	$5.99		
☐ *Instant Family Fitness* — A parent's guide to keeping your family healthy & happy	$5.99		
Postage & Handling: U.S., $ 2.75 for one book, $ 1.00 for each additional			
Total enclosed:			

Ship to:

NAME _____

ADDRESS _____

CITY _____ STATE _____ ZIP _____

Please make your check or money order payable to AMI Books and mail it along with this order form to AMI Mail Order Books, 1000 American Media Way, Boca Raton, FL 33464-1000. Allow 4-6 weeks for delivery. Payable in U.S. funds only. No cash or COD accepted. We accept check or money orders ($15.00 fee for returned check). **Offer not available in Canada.**

1204CYL